Getting Started

with

WordPerfect® 5.1

Wiley PC Companions

Gips: MASTERING LOTUS 1-2-3, Release 2.2, A Problem Solving Approach
Wiley: GETTING STARTED WITH dBASE III PLUS, Extended (Student Version Available)
Wiley: GETTING STARTED WITH LOTUS 1-2-3, Release 2.2
Wiley: GETTING STARTED WITH WORDPERFECT 4.2/5.0, Extended (Student Version Available)
Wiley: GETTING STARTED WITH WORDPERFECT 5.1
Wiley: EXPLORING DOS, WORDPERFECT 5.1, LOTUS 1-2-3, RELEASE 2.2 AND dBASE III PLUS
Sachs: DISCOVERING MICROSOFT WORKS—IBM PC (Student Version Available)
Sachs: DISCOVERING MICROSOFT WORKS—Projects, Applications and Exercises
Spezzano: ENABLE 2.14: THE FUNDAMENTALS (Student Version Available)
Spezzano: ENABLE 2.14: ADVANCED TOPICS (Student Version Available)
Stern: GETTING STARTED WITH dBASE III PLUS (Student Version Included)
Stern: GETTING STARTED WITH VP-PLANNER
Stern: GETTING STARTED WITH WORDPERFECT 4.2 (Student Version Included)
Stern: GETTING STARTED WITH MS-DOS
Stern: COMPUTING APPLICATIONS USING DOS, WORDPERFECT 5.0, LOTUS 1-2-3 AND dBASE IV
Stern: GETTING STARTED WITH BASIC

Wiley Macintosh Companions

Abernethy, Nanney and Porter: EXPLORING MACINTOSH: Concepts In Visually Oriented Computing
Nanney, Porter and Abernethy: EXPLORING MICROSOFT WORKS 2.0—Macintosh

Getting Started with WordPerfect® 5.1

Jerry Murphy
Oregon State System of Higher Education

WILEY
John Wiley and Sons
New York Chichester Brisbane Toronto Singapore

Trademark Acknowledgments:

1-2-3 is a registered trademark of Lotus Development Corporation
dBASE III PLUS is a registered trademark of Ashton-Tate Corporation
IBM is a registered trademark of International Business Machines Corp.
Lotus is a registered trademark of Lotus Development Corporation
MS-DOS is a registered trademark of Microsoft Corporation
WordPerfect is a registered trademark of WordPerfect Corporation

ISBN 0-471-53378-5 (5.25 inch version)
ISBN 0-471-54429-9 (3.5 inch version)

Printed in the United States of America

Printed and bound by Port City Press, Inc.

10 9 8 7 6

Sponsoring Editor: Joe Dougherty, John Wiley & Sons, Inc.
Production Services by BMR, Corte Madera, CA
Copy Edit: Dale Nicholls
Cover Design: Kenny Beck
Development Edit: Susan Maunders
Index: BevAnne Ross
Page Makeup: Carol A. Martin
Production Coordination: Nancy Taylor Mason
Text Design: Barbara B. Gelfand

CONTENTS

Lesson 11 Importing Spreadsheets

Lesson 12 Equations

PREFACE

This tutorial provides step-by-step instructions on how to use WordPerfect commands quickly and easily to create reports, letters, and documents. The lessons are arranged so that essential material is presented first, followed by advanced material—the exciting and powerful features that make
WordPerfect such a popular word processor.

After completing the first lesson you should begin to satisfy 70 to 75 percent of your word processing needs. After you complete the second lesson, you should be able to satisfy 80 to 85 percent of all of your basic word processing needs. When you have completed the essential part, the first six lessons, you should be able to satisfy about 95 percent of your word processing needs. The essential commands are basic to using WordPerfect, so you might consider completing each of the first six lessons twice to make sure you can remember the commands without looking them up.

The advanced topics covered in lessons 7 to 12 are loosely arranged in order of importance, but you can execute them in any order you choose. Your own need to develop competence in a given topic will most likely determine the sequence in which you complete these advanced lessons. As you work with the individual advanced topics, you will probably tell yourself how easy the program is, and note what spectacular results it produces.

The exercises at the end of each lesson are arranged to build upon problems from previous lessons. For example, with the exception of Lesson 1, all of the Group A Accounting problems at the end of each lesson depend upon the previous lesson's work. The same is true for each of the defined groups of problems. Once you have learned how to word process, you will probably wonder how you ever got along without it.

I

Introduction

Hardware Needed

- IBM PC, IBM PS/2, or IBM PC-compatible microcomputer
- Dual 360K-byte or 720K-byte floppy-disk drives or hard drive with one 360K-byte or 720K-byte floppy-disk drive

Software Needed

- DOS 2.0 or later version
- WordPerfect 5.1
- Student data disk with files

What Is WordPerfect 5.1?

Word processing has revolutionized the modern office by giving individual workers many of the capabilities of a typesetting business. Students, too, can create professional-quality documents with word processing programs. A particularly versatile and user-friendly program is WordPerfect 5.1. This tutorial will help you learn to use the program with IBM PC and compatible equipment to produce professional-looking documents more quickly and easily.

WordPerfect allows the user to create and revise a document right at the keyboard. By using the appropriate command, you can

- Move copy within a document
- Insert copy from one document into another document
- Delete copy
- Check spelling
- Change the margins, spacing and other format features
- Integrate diagrams, figures, and tabular matter—including material created on other programs, such as spreadsheet and graphic programs—with text material

WordPerfect graphics can produce the following types of visual images:

- Boxes for equations to create and display the unusual mathematical symbols not normally found on the keyboard
- Boxes for figures to display charts, clip art, and diagrams
- Boxes for tables to display lists or tables of numerical values
- Boxes for text to display text material given special treatment such as quotes, sidebars, and special documentation
- Boxes created by the user to display an image not conforming to any of the first 4 types of boxes
- Horizontal and vertical lines positioned for special effects

You can place the graphics boxes and lines in specific positions on the paper. In addition, you can place text around the boxes if you choose. In some instances, the versatile graphics box will allow you to turn the material on its side, flip it over, reverse the image, or turn it upside down.

Additionally, spreadsheets created in other spreadsheet programs can be made a part of the document. Other notable features allow you to create tables and rearrange lines and paragraphs. Features which were the exclusive domain of typesetting a few years ago can now be accomplished in WordPerfect 5.1.

Once you become familiar with the program, you may well wonder how you ever survived without it!

The WordPerfect Keyboard

To use WordPerfect to the fullest advantage, take a few minutes to locate important keys such as Control [Ctrl], Alternate [Alt], Escape [Esc], Delete [Delete], Enter [Enter], and other special function keys on your keyboard as shown in Figure I-1.

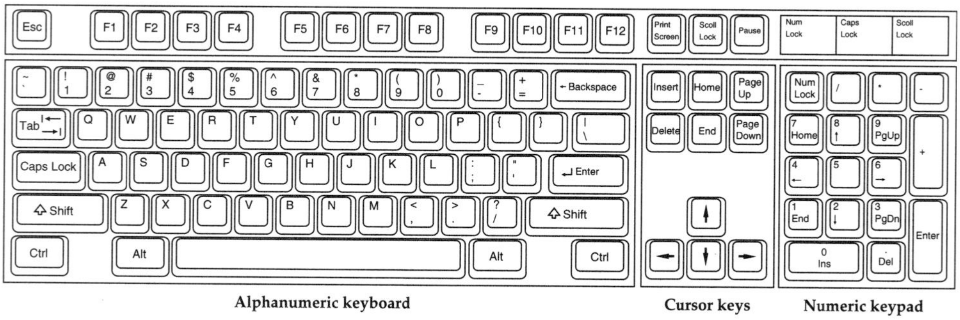

Figure I-1:
Keyboard

There are generally two different types of keyboards. The IBM PC and XT keyboards have the special function keys [F1] to [F10] located in two vertical columns on the left side of the keyboard. The PC/AT and PS/2 keyboards have the special function keys [F1] to [F12] located along the top of the keyboard. The latter keyboard is known as a 101 keyboard because of its 101 keys. Learning the keyboard is especially important because WordPerfect is designed so that each key can be used to make word processing quick and convenient.

[Alt], [Ctrl], and [Shift]

Pay particular attention to the [Alt], [Ctrl], and [Shift] keys in Figure I-1. These keys normally do nothing when pressed by themselves. They are always used in combination with a second key—such as a function key—to give that key a meaning it would not have by itself. A possible exception is the [Alt] key, which can be programmed to retrieve WordPerfect's pull-down menus when pressed and then released before any other key is struck. (The pull-down menus will be discussed in more detail in Lesson 1.)

The Function Keys

Each of the [F1] to [F10] function keys has four distinct uses in WordPerfect, depending on whether it is used by itself or in combination with [Shift], [Alt], or [Ctrl]. To use one of the combinations, press the [Shift], [Alt], or [Ctrl] key first and continue holding it down while striking the appropriate function key once. Such key combinations are shown in the tutorial with a plus sign (+). If the tutorial instructs you to execute **[Shift]+[F8]**, press the shift key and hold it down while you strike **[F8]** once. What would you do in response to the instruction **[Ctrl]+[F2]**?

The 101 keyboard has two additional function keys: the [F11] and [F12] keys. The two extra function keys are not normally used in combination with any other key. With a single stroke, each of these two keys duplicates a special word processing feature that is produced by a combination of other function keys on the smaller keyboard. The two single-use features are Reveal Codes [F11] and Block [F12].

The [Enter] Key

The [Enter], or [Return], key is the large gray key located just above the right-hand [Shift] key on the keyboard. In this tutorial, we refer to it as the [Enter] key.

When typing text in WordPerfect, you do not need to strike the [Enter] key at the end of the line on the screen. The [Enter] key does not work like the carriage return key on a typewriter. When there is no more space on the current line, the computer automatically sends the cursor to the beginning of the next line. This word processing feature is called word-wrap.

You will usually use the [Enter] key to end a paragraph or to produce blank lines.

The Template Color Scheme

The WordPerfect function-key template, supplied with the software, fits around the PC/XT function keys or above the 101 keyboard function keys. The purpose of the template is to remind you of what each key or combination of keys generates. The template uses a color scheme to identify which key or keys produce the forty unique word processing operations for [F1] through [F10] and their combinations with [Shift], [Ctrl], and [Alt]. The template works like this:

Red When a function is listed in red on the template, use the function key with the **[Ctrl]** key. For example, to use WordPerfect's spell-checker, press **[Ctrl]+[F2]**. Notice the word **Spell** shown in red on the template, by the [F2] key.

Green When a name is listed in green, use the function key with the **[Shift]** key.

Blue When a name is listed in blue, use the function key with the **[Alt]** key.

Black When a name is listed in black, use the function key **alone**.

Entering WordPerfect

Start your computer and use the DOS commands to go to the drive that will access the WordPerfect software. If you are unsure how to turn on your system and use DOS commands, you should review the *GETTING STARTED WITH: MS-DOS* tutorial before attempting this tutorial.

Dual Disk Drive Machines

To run WordPerfect 5.1 using a two-disk system, each floppy-disk drive must have a capacity of at least 360K bytes.

To start WordPerfect 5.1 on a dual disk drive computer,

1. ....Insert the MS-DOS or PC-DOS disk into drive A and turn on the computer.
2. ....At the prompt **Enter New Date:**, type the current date and press **[Enter]**.
3. ....At the prompt **Enter New Time:**, type the correct time and press **[Enter]**.
4. ....Remove the DOS disk from drive A and insert the WordPerfect Program 1 disk into drive B.

5. . . . .Insert the student data disk in drive A.
6. . . . .To start WordPerfect, type **B:wp** and press **[Enter].**
7. . . . .At the prompt, replace the WordPerfect Program 1 disk with the WordPerfect Program 2 disk.

If you have successfully started WordPerfect 5.1, a brief message on the screen will tell you that WordPerfect 5.1 has been accessed. The screen will then change to appear as Figure I-2. You are now ready to start the first lesson of the tutorial.

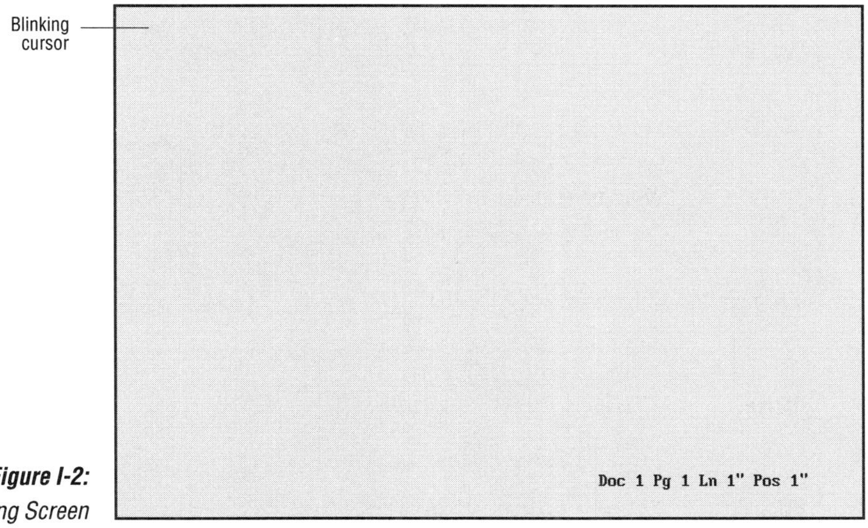

Figure I-2:
Beginning Screen

If an error message appears instead of a screen like that shown in Figure I-2, see the section on "Startup Messages" that follows.

Hard Disk Drive Machines

Go to the directory where WordPerfect is stored. Each network system has its own procedures. See your Network Manager for the correct procedure to access the WordPerfect 5.1 program.

1. . . . .Type **WP** and press **[Enter]**

If you have succeeded in starting WordPerfect, you will briefly see a message on the screen telling you that WordPerfect 5.1 has been accessed. After a few seconds, the screen will change to look like the screen shown in Figure I-2. You are now ready to start the first lesson of the tutorial.

If an error message appears instead of a screen like that shown in Figure I-2, see the section on "Startup Messages" that follows.

Startup Messages

If you see a message such as **Invalid directory** or **Bad command or file name**, the WordPerfect 5.1 program is probably located in a different directory or disk drive than the one you are using, or the command may have been misspelled.

The message **Drive not ready reading drive A. 1 Retry: 2 Cancel: 1** means that the WordPerfect 5.1 program is requesting you insert the WordPerfect 5.1 disk into disk drive A or is telling you that the drive door needs to be closed. Insert your disk and press **1** or close the disk drive door and press **1**.

The message **Are other copies of WordPerfect currently running? (Y/N)** is normally displayed when WordPerfect was previously exited improperly in a single-user environment. Press **N** to continue.

1

Starting Up

The objectives of this lesson are to

- Identify the status line
- Erase text with the **[Delete]** and **[Backspace]** keys
- Move the cursor
- Enter text
- Use word-wrap
- Save a document
- Spell-check a document
- Print a document
- View a document before printing
- Exit from WordPerfect
- Clear the screen
- Introduce the pull-down menus

Identifying the Status Line

Load WordPerfect 5.1, following the steps given in the Introduction. Your screen should now be blank except for a line of information in the lower-right corner and a blinking cursor in the upper-left corner as shown in Figure 1-1. The cursor is a small underline character that marks the position where the next character you type will appear. The line of information in the lower right is called the **status line.** The status line's primary purpose is to provide information about the cursor's current location, but it sometimes provides messages, warnings, and other prompts. At times, the status line provides a menu for you to select from or indicates an action you must perform to enable the program to continue.

Using the [Backspace] Key

Striking the [Backspace] key will immediately erase the character to the left of the cursor. If you catch a mistake immediately or shortly after you make

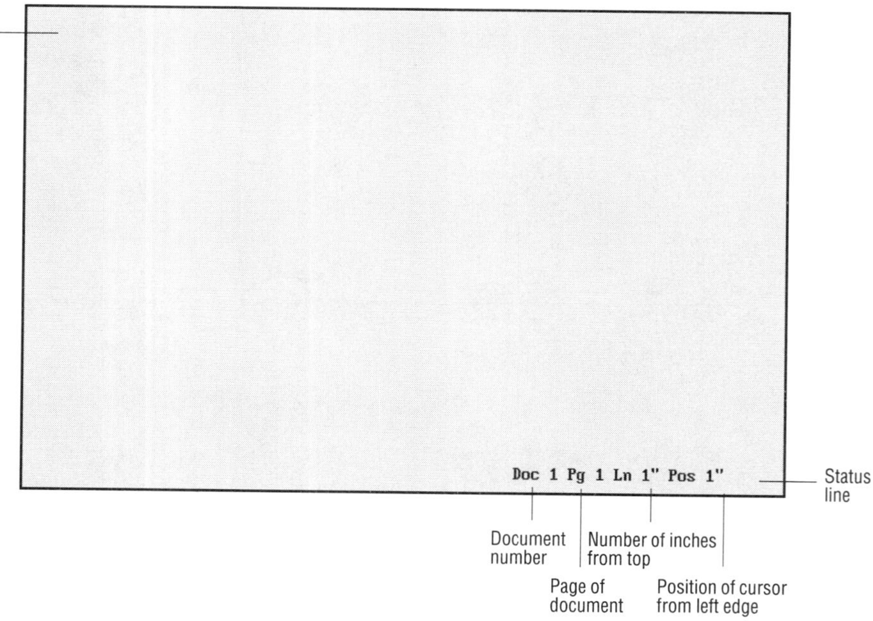

Figure 1-1: *Beginning Screen Components*

it, you can erase the error by striking the [Backspace] key. Then you can continue to insert text.

The [Backspace] key will continuously repeat the backspacing and erasing function as long as it is held down. Multiple adjacent keystrokes to the left of the cursor can be erased by holding the [Backspace] key down until you have erased all of the error.

You may also use the [Backspace] key with the [Ctrl] key to erase. With the cursor positioned at any character in a word, you can erase the entire word by holding down the [Ctrl] key and striking the [Backspace] key.

Using the [Delete] Key

The [Delete], or [Del], key erases the character at the position of the cursor and shifts all text to the right of the cursor one space to the left. The [Delete] key also has the repeat function and it will continue to delete characters at the position of the cursor until it is released.

You may also use the [Delete] key with the [Ctrl] key to erase entire words. With the cursor positioned at any character in a word, you can erase the word by holding down the [Ctrl] key and striking the [Delete] key.

Moving the Cursor

WordPerfect has a large variety of keys that you can use for cursor movement. You can move character by character or line by line using only the **up** [↑], **down** [↓], **left** [←], and **right** [→] arrow keys. With a few keystrokes you can move word by word, to the beginning or end of a line, to the top or bottom of the screen or the page, and all the way to the beginning or end of a document. These movements, shown in Table 1-1, will become automatic for you.

In the following cursor movement commands, the plus sign (+) between key symbols means hold the left key down while striking the second key one time and then release the first key.

Entering Text

To see how WordPerfect works, try entering some text.

1.....Type the three paragraphs shown in Figure 1-2.

Figure 1-2: *WordPerfect 5.1 Features*

> WordPerfect 5.1 is one of the most powerful and comprehensive word processing programs available. It is fast, efficient, and a genuine pleasure to use. However, the program is better known for an abundance of helpful features and the fact that WordPerfect Corporation keeps making each version more proficient.
>
> WordPerfect 5.1 offers all of the fundamental word processing functions, such as automatic word-wrap, which creates a new line when the cursor reaches the right margin and moves the cursor down to the new line, and automatic rewrite, which automatically reformats your paragraphs after any editing changes, such as adding or deleting text through keyboard entry or using search and replace commands to locate and/or change a word or phrase.
>
> WordPerfect 5.1 has capabilities that extend way beyond the basics to include special features, including a pull-down menu, a spell-checker, a thesaurus, automatic footnotes and endnotes, newspaper columns, and alphabetical and numeric sorting. Additionally, it allows you to create ghraphics, spreadsheets, macros, line drawings, equations, and mathematical functions to perform addition, subtraction, multiplication, division, and averaging.

As you type, do not press the [Enter] key until the end of each paragraph—let word-wrap end the lines for you automatically. You may need to use the [Backspace] key and [Delete] key while entering the text to correct any mistakes.

Proofreading Your Text

Now that you have entered all of the text, proofread the material for typing errors. If you have typing errors in the document, move the cursor to the appropriate position and make the necessary corrections with the [Backspace] or [Del] keys.

WP 10

Cursor Movement Commands

Pressing these keys:	Moves the cursor:
Up [↑] arrow	Up 1 line
Down [↓] arrow	Down 1 line
Left [←] arrow	Left 1 character
Right [→] arrow	Right 1 character
[Ctrl]+[←]	One word to the left
[Ctrl]+[→]	One word to the right
[Home], [←]	Left edge of current line
[Home], [→] (or [End] key)	Right edge of currrent line
[Home], [↑] (or minus key)	One screen up
[Home], [↓] (or plus key)	One screen down
[PgUp]	Top of previous page
[PgDn]	Top of next page
[Home], [Home], [↑]	Top of document
[Home], [Home], [↓]	End of document
[Home], [Home], [→]	Far right edge of document
[Home], [Home], [←]	Far left edge of document
[Home], [Home], [Home], [↑]	Top of document before any code
[Home], [Home], [Home], [←]	Far left of line before any code
[Esc], any number (n), [→]	n spaces to the right
[Esc], any number (n), [←]	n spaces to the left
[Esc], any number (n), [PgUp]	n pages up from current page
[Esc], any number (n), [PgDn]	n pages down from current page
[Ctrl]+[Home], any number	To that page number
[Ctrl]+[Home], [↑]	Top of current page
[Ctrl]+[Home], [↓]	End of current page
[Ctrl]+[Home], any letter A-Z or a-z, digit, or special character	Next occurrence of that letter, digit, or special character

NOTE: Keystrokes separated by commas mean press and release the keys sequentially; these keys so labeled are not to be pressed together.

Table 1-1: *Cursor Movement Commands*

Saving Your Document

Although you can see your document on the screen, it actually exists only in your computer's on-line memory (RAM) and is not permanent until you save it to a disk. Because on-line memory disappears as soon as the computer is turned off, it is essential that you save your document to a disk file if you ever want to use it again.

With the student data disk in drive A,

1. . . . . Press **[F10]** (Save)
   You should see the following prompt on the status line:
   Document to be saved:

2. . . . . Type **A:LESSON1** and press **[Enter]**
   Do not leave a space between the "N" of LESSON and the digit 1. The "A:" saves the document to your student data disk in drive A.

In creating file names, WordPerfect uses the DOS file-naming conventions. You can use any of the following characters to create up to an eight-character name followed by an optional three-character extension name (_ _ _ _ _ _ _ _._ _ _):

A-Z
0-9
! @ # $ % & ( ) - ' ' { }

All other characters on the keyboard, including the spacebar and the asterisk (*), are unacceptable for use in a file name.

If you use DOS 3.0 or later versions, you can use international characters in file names. You cannot use graphics characters.

NOTE: In WordPerfect, do not use the three character extensions .COM, .EXE, or .WPM. These extensions are reserved for program and WordPerfect macro files. If you accidentally name a file with one of the "not to be used" extensions, rename the file.

The optional extension name starts with a period followed by one to three valid characters. If you type lowercase alphabetic characters, they are automatically changed to uppercase when the save command is executed.

Using the Spell-Checker

A mechanical way to proofread your material is to retrieve the spell-checker by using the command **[Ctrl]+[F2]** and letting the computer check the spelling. You can check the spelling of a word, or the spelling in the current page, or in the entire current document. If the spell-checker finds a word that it cannot identify, you will be asked to select an option from the menu. From the menu, you can skip the word, or select the correct spelling, or edit the word to the correct spelling; or you can add words which are not in the vocabulary, such as JIT, which is an acronym you will encounter in the Group D Production exercises.

To check the spelling of all of the words in the current document,

1. . . . .Press **[Ctrl]+[F2]**
The following menu will appear:
Check: 1 **W**ord; 2 **P**age; 3 **D**ocument;

2. . . . .Press **3** to check the spelling in your document.
If a word is highlighted as misspelled, choose one of the options presented on the screen.
3. . . . .Press [Enter] to leave the spell-checker.

NOTE: The spell-checker cannot identify as an error a word that is correctly spelled but that is the wrong word for its context: for example, "than" instead of "then." Nor can it identify omitted words or incorrect punctuation. Incorrect punctuation can be handled by a separate grammar-check program but all of the remaining grammatical errors still require a human to identify the error.

If you locate and correct one or more errors, save the corrected text by repeating the previous command for saving a file, and answering **Y**es to the **Replace?** prompt.

Using the Print Command

You can invoke the Print command **[Shift]+[F7]** at any time and from any place within the document. Pressing the key combination results in a screen like the one shown in Figure 1-3.

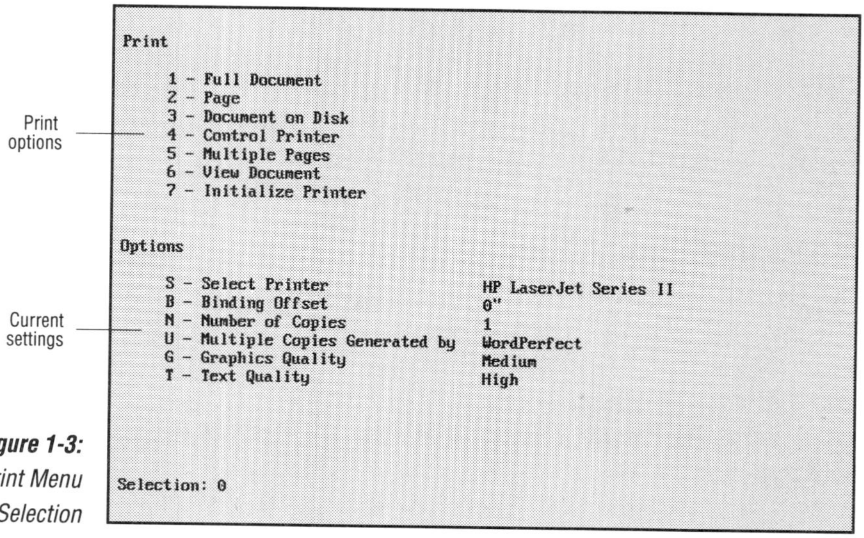

Figure 1-3: *Print Menu Selection*

To print the current document,

1.....Press **[Shift]+[F7]**, **1** to select the Full Document option.

NOTE: The printer must be connected and turned on.

Viewing the Document

At any time, you can summon a preview of the document to be printed by choosing the View Document option **6** of the Print command. You can also use the View option to aid in the placement of material on the page prior to printing. The View option displays exactly what the printer will produce when you invoke the Print command.

To view text and graphics placement on the current document,

1.....Press **[Shift]+[F7]**, **6** to select the View Document option.

The following submenu will appear on the status line:

1 100% **2** 200% **3** Full Page **4** Facing Pages: **3** **Doc 1 Pg 1**

These submenu options perform the following functions:

Option	Screen Result
1	Displays the current page of the document in the same size it will be printed
2	Displays the current page twice as large as it will be printed
3	Displays all of the current page in reduced size
4	Displays the left and right pages of the document as in an open book; shows even-numbered pages on the left, and odd-numbered pages on the right

You can use the **[PgUp]** and **[PgDn]** keys to view other pages of a multi-page document. You can use the other arrow cursor movement keys in modes 1 and 2 to examine parts of the current page that are not initially visible on the screen. You can switch between the four modes while in the View mode.

To return to the document in the Edit mode,

2.....Press the spacebar twice.

Exiting from WordPerfect

To exit from WordPerfect, press **[F7]**. When you have executed this command, the system will ask you in a prompt if you want to save the current document. If you saved the document previously and have not made any changes to it, there will be a second prompt in the lower right corner on the status line informing you that the text has not been modified since the last save command.

To exit from WordPerfect and save the current document,

1.....Press **[F7]**
The prompt will say
Save document? Yes (**N**o)

2.....Press **[Enter]**
Because the document had been saved previously, the following prompt appears:
Document to be saved: A:\LESSON1

3.....Press **[Enter]**
The prompt will say
Replace A:\LESSON1? No (**Y**es)

4.....Press **Y**
The message **Saving A:\LESSON1** will appear until the saving is completed. When the following prompt appears:
Exit WP? No (**Y**es) (**Cancel** to return to document)

5.....Press **[F1]**
You will be returned to the document you were working on.

Do not choose the Yes option until you have completed questions 1, 2, and 3 in the practice exercises.

Clearing the Screen

Any time you want to erase the screen (delete the file from the on-line memory) and start work on a new lesson or document, you need to use the Exit **[F7]** key. Do not clear the screen at this time. The procedure is similar to the first three steps for exiting WordPerfect. If you were to clear the screen, at the prompt
Exit WP? No (**Y**es) (**Cancel** to return to document)

1.....You would press **N**
The screen would then be blank except for the status line in the lower right corner.

To verify that the screen has been cleared, you would press any of the cursor movement keys. The cursor could not move because the screen is blank! This illustrates an important concept in WordPerfect: the cursor can move only through existing text or through blank space created by pressing [Enter].

Using the Pull-Down Menus

WordPerfect 5.1 has the added feature of pull-down menus. The pull-down menus are activated by pressing **[Alt]+[=]**. This feature is probably best used after you have become familiar with the specific keystrokes for a command. Knowing how to activate the pull-down menus does not negate the need to know the specific sequence of keys required to complete the command. There are some problems in using the menus without knowing the keystrokes.

The pull-down menus will allow you to start any of the commands, but if additional keystrokes are required to complete the procedure, you will have to execute the process just as you would in the original key-in method. Note that using the pull-down menus usually takes longer than using the key-in method.

Another difficulty encountered at first in using the pull-down menus is trying to remember which option in the main menu contains the command you wish to use. The pull-down menus are faster only when you do not need to use the reference manual to help you locate commands in the menus. Thus, the pull-down menus are most useful when you need help with simple commands.

Because it is difficult to use the pull-down menus in the early stages of learning of WordPerfect, this tutorial does not cover the feature in depth.

General Exercises

If you have exited from WordPerfect, see the section, "Retrieving a Document," (on page 20) in Lesson 2 to retrieve your LESSON1 file.

1. Experiment with moving the cursor around the LESSON1 file using each of the keystroke combinations.
2. Retrieve the spell-checker and experiment with options 1, 2, 3, and 6.
3. Using the cursor movement commands, go to **a** / in the text. Also try to locate the following individual characters: semicolon (;) C c P z 4 comma (,) period (.).
4. If you intend to go on to another set of exercises, clear the screen. If not, exit WordPerfect. Do not save any of this practice exercise material.

Course-Specific Exercises

Group A Accounting

1. If you have exited from WordPerfect, load it and type the following text. Temporarily ignore any typing errors.

   Accounting is the process of providing financial information to those who must control and manage scarce resources: labor, materials, and capital. Accounting includes activities such as recording, summarizing, reporting, and interpreting financial data. The function of accounting is to provide quantitative financial information for use in making economic decisions.

Accounting information provides the basis for economic decisions both inside and outside business enterprises. Because of their financial knowledge, accountants are often asked to search through the available financial data for clues which will serve as guides to the future.

The accounting information is essential to the decision-making system of a firm, because it provides quantitative information for the three functions of planning, control, and evaluation. Without the detailed and accurate financial information provided by accountants, no sound and reliable decision-making system could be developed.

2. Use the spell-checker to check the document.
3. How many words does the accounting document contain?
4. Using the cursor movement commands, have the computer locate a hyphen (-) in the text. Also try to locate the following individual characters: semicolon (;) A a P x 3 period (.).
5. Save the file as A:ACCTG.ONE.
6. If you intend to go on to another set of exercises, clear the screen. If not, exit WordPerfect.

Group B Marketing

1. Load WordPerfect if necessary. Type the following text. Temporarily ignore any typing errors.

   Marketing is the process of planning and executing the conception, pricing, promotion, and distribution of ideas, goods, and services to create exchanges that will satisfy individual and organizational objectives.

   Marketing is concerned with satisfying the wants and needs of specific subgroups of consumers. The specific subgroup to which a marketing program directs its attention is called a target market. A firm must develop a marketing plan that satisfies the needs of the targeted group of buyers.

   With a focus on a target market, a firm's marketing department works with a combination of factors to sell the product. The four factors controlled by the firm to market the product are known as the four P's: (1) product, (2) place, (3) price, and (4) promotion. These four factors are called the "marketing mix."

2. Use the spell-checker to check the document.
3. How many words does the marketing document contain?

4. Using the cursor movement commands, have the computer locate a colon (:) in the text. Also try to locate the following individual characters: semicolon (;) M m T y 4) period (.).
5. Save the file as A:MARKTING.ONE.
6. If you intend to go on to another set of exercises, clear the screen. If not, exit WordPerfect.

Group C Finance

1. Load WordPerfect if necessary. Type the following text. Temporarily ignore any typing errors.

   The function of financial management is to plan for, acquire, and utilize funds in a way which maximizes the value of the firm. Finance is concerned with evaluating and acquiring productive assets, procuring the least expensive mix of funds, and disbursing profits in a manner consistent with the best interests of the firm's owners.

   High inflation, high interest rates, limited resources, and increased international competition have created the need for new and innovative financial management of a firm's resources. The financial manager now has more direct responsibility for overseeing the control process as opposed to merely raising the money needed to purchase such things as a plant, equipment or inventories.

   The financial manager must determine the investment, financing, and dividend policies of the firm. The assumption is that management's primary goal is to maximize the wealth of its stockholders. This translates into maximizing the price of common stock.

2. Use the spell-checker to check the document.
3. How many words does the finance document contain?
4. Using the cursor movement commands, have the computer locate an apostrophe (') in the text. Also try to locate the following individual characters: semicolon (;) F f P M z period (.).
5. Save the file as A:FINANCE.ONE.
6. If you intend to go on to another set of exercises, clear the screen. If not, exit WordPerfect.

Group D Production

1. Load WordPerfect if necessary. Type the following text. Temporarily ignore any typing errors.

   It is appropriate that Just-In-Time (JIT) be considered as a way of doing business because the savings and the improvements which can be accrued from its adoption as a company philosophy are significant. Tektronix's Wilsonville plant can be cited as an example of the savings and the improvements resulting from JIT. Eighteen months after implementing JIT, the Wilsonville plant had (1) reduced inventory by

74%; (2) reduced manufacturing lead time by 91%; (3) reduced stockroom floor space by 57%; and (4) increased productivity by 37%.

JIT can be defined as the relentless pursuit of the reduction of waste through enforced problem solving. Utilizing this definition, manufacturers can use JIT to obtain major gains in productivity, reduce manufacturing costs, and gain the ability to react to rapidly changing demand patterns.

When an organization changes its manufacturing philosophy, it requires a "champion" to see the change through to completion. JIT is no exception. It requires the leadership of an extremely confident manager who is committed to the success of the changeover and who has the ability to see that the philosophy is started and continued throughout the company.

2. Use the spell-checker to check the document.
3. How many words does the production document contain?
4. Using the cursor movement commands, have the computer locate a semicolon (;) in the text. Also try to locate the following individual characters: I i J z 9 comma (,) period (.).
5. Save the file as A:PRODUCT.ONE and exit WordPerfect.

2

Enhancing the Document

The objectives of this lesson are to

- Cancel a command
- Escape from a procedure
- Retrieve an existing file from disk
- Use the help feature
- Center text
- Use the Reveal Codes command
- Change left- and right-hand margins
- Change top and bottom margins
- Change line justification
- Change line height and line spacing
- Create underlined and bold text

Canceling a Command

Occasionally, when you use the keyboard keys for a WordPerfect function or command, you may accidentally press the wrong key or keys. When this happens, you can use the Cancel **[F1]** function key.

The [F1] function key cancels almost all commands. Even when you have already chosen options within a command, using the [F1] key will allow you to start all over on either the same command or a different command. However, note that you can cancel the Reveal Codes command only by issuing the Reveal Codes command a second time. The Cancel function key will not work on the Reveal Codes command.

Using the [Escape] Key

The Escape **[Esc]** key is similar to the [F1] key in that you can use it to cancel a command which you have already invoked. The [Esc] key works best just after the command has been invoked but not yet used or completed.

Unlike the Cancel key, the [Esc] key can be used with the [Delete] key to delete characters, words, lines, and pages. However, the [Backspace] and [Delete] keys are easier to use and control, and are better choices for deleting small groups of either words or characters. The [Esc] key is best used to cancel a command and to perform those functions shown in Table 2-1.

Special Escape Key Functions

Keystrokes	Action Performed
[Esc], n, [Ctrl]+[End]	Deletes n lines from the right of the cursor.
[Esc], n, [Ctrl]+[PgDn]	Deletes n pages beginning with the page the cursor is on.
[Esc], n, (any character)	Inserts n copies of the character beginning at the position of the cursor.

Table 2-1: *Escape Key Functions*
Listing of

Retrieving a Document

Because you saved the LESSON1 document in the previous lesson, you can now retrieve it to the screen.

To retrieve LESSON1,

1.....Press **[Shift]+[F10]**
You should see the following prompt on the status line:
Document to be retrieved:

2.....Type **A:LESSON1** and press **[Enter]**
The three paragraphs you typed in LESSON1 should appear on your screen, unless you misspelled the name or did not save the file in the previous lesson. If you see the **ERROR file not found** message, type the file name again with the correct spelling.

Using the List Files Key

Word processing often provides more than one way to accomplish a particular function. For example, WordPerfect gives you more than one procedure for retrieving a stored file. In the previous section, you learned how to retrieve a document by pressing **[Shift]+[F10]** and typing the file name. But what do you do when you cannot remember the file name, or are unsure of how it is spelled? For this situation, WordPerfect provides the List Files **[F5]** key to help retrieve documents.

Clear the screen using the [F7] key. To retrieve your LESSON1 file using the List Files [F5] key,

1.....Press **[F5]**

Your status line may say

DIR C:\WP51*.* (Type = to change default Dir)

With your student data disk in drive A,

2. . . . .Press **=** to let WordPerfect know that you want to change the default drive from C to A.

To continue,

3. . . . .Type **A:** and press **[Enter] [Enter]**

You will see a list of all file names on your student data disk in the A drive, like the list shown in Figure 2-1.

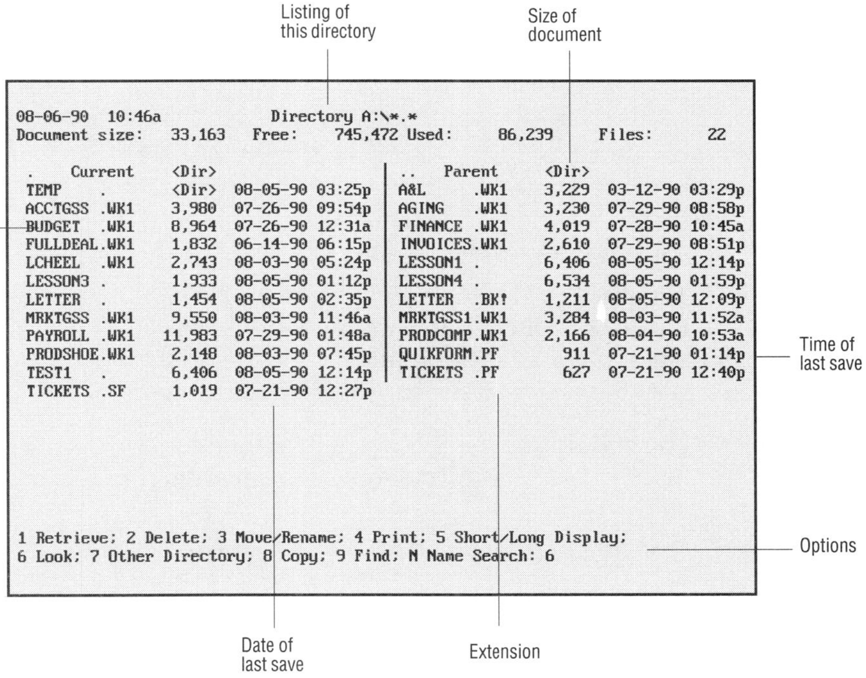

Figure 2-1: *Result of List Files Command*

Several menu options at the bottom of the screen let you retrieve a file, copy files, delete files, and more. Use the arrow keys to move the highlighted area onto the file you saved earlier, LESSON1.

4. . . . .Press **1**

The List Files menu disappears and the file, LESSON1, appears on the screen again.

You can now begin to practice inserting text into a WordPerfect document. In this exercise you will insert your name at the top of the document. To insure that the cursor is at the top of the document,

1. . . . .Press **[Home] [Home] [↑]**

2. . . . .Press **[Enter] [Enter]**

Notice that the entire document and the cursor move down two lines. When the cursor is at the left margin, pressing the [Enter] key inserts a blank line above the cursor.

Now move the cursor to line 1 of the document. (Check the status line for position of the cursor.)

3.....Type (**your name**) and press **[Enter]**

Your name should now appear at the top of the document.

Using the Help Feature

The amount of on-line help available to the user in a piece of software is one measure of how user-friendly the program is. WordPerfect provides an enormous amount of help through the keyboard. To request the Help feature, press the **[F3]** key.

If you misplace the keyboard template for the function keys, you can access a picture of the template by pressing **[F3]** twice. If you have access to a graphics printer you can print what you see on the screen by pressing the **[PrtSc]** key.

When you know what function you want to execute but cannot tell from the template exactly where the function is located, you can press **[F3]** and then press the first letter of the desired operation. For example, if you cannot locate or read the command for centering the typed material of the LESSON1 file between the top and bottom margins, access the Help feature.

1.....Press **[F3]**

Then, to see the information on centering,

2.....Press **C**

You will see a screen like the one shown in Figure 2-2.

Features [C]	WordPerfect Key	Keystrokes
Cancel	Cancel	F1
Cancel Hyphenation Code	Home	Home,/
Cancel Print Job(s)	Print	Shft-F7,4,1
Capitalize Block (Block On)	Switch	Shft-F3,1
Cartridges and Fonts	Print	Shft-F7,s,3,4
Case Conversion (Block On)	Switch	Shft-F3
Center Block (Block On)	Center	Shft-F6
Center Justification	Format	Shft-F8,1,3,2
Center Page (Top to Bottom)	Format	Shft-F8,2,1
Center Tab Setting	Format	Shft-F8,1,8,c
Center Text	Center	Shft-F6
Centered Text With Dot Leaders	Center	Shft-F6,Shft-F6
Centimeters, Units of Measure	Setup	Shft-F1,3,8
Change Comment to Text	Text In/Out	Ctrl-F5,4,3
Change Default Directory	List	F5,=,Dir name,Enter
Change Font	Font	Ctrl-F8
Change Supplementary Dictionary	Spell	Ctrl-F2,4
Change Text to Comment (Block On)	Text In/Out	Shft-F5
Character Sets	Compose	Ctrl-v or Ctrl-2
Character Spacing	Format	Shft-F8,4,6,3
More... Press c to continue.		
Selection: 0		(Press ENTER to exit Help)

Figure 2-2: *Help Screen*

The Help screen indicates you should press **[Shift]+[F8]**, **2**, **1** to center the typed material between top and bottom margins.

3. . . . .Press **[Enter]** to leave Help.

Centering a Page

Because WordPerfect commands affect only the material which appears after the command, position the cursor at the top of the document and

1. . . . .Press **[Shift]+[F8]**
From the menu (as shown in Figure 2-3),

```
Format

     1 - Line
              Hyphenation                    Line Spacing
              Justification                  Margins Left/Right
              Line Height                    Tab Set
              Line Numbering                 Widow/Orphan Protection

     2 - Page
              Center Page (top to bottom)    Page Numbering
              Force Odd/Even Page            Paper Size/Type
              Headers and Footers            Suppress
              Margins Top/Bottom

     3 - Document
              Display Pitch                  Redline Method
              Initial Codes/Font             Summary

     4 - Other
              Advance                        Overstrike
              Conditional End of Page        Printer Functions
              Decimal Characters             Underline Spaces/Tabs
              Language

Selection: 0
```

Figure 2-3: *Document Format Menu*

2. . . . .Press **2** to select Page.
From the menu shown in Figure 2-4,
3. . . . .Press **1**
4. . . . .Press **Y** to automatically center the paragraphs between the top and bottom margins.
5. . . . .Press **[Enter] [Enter]** to return to your document.

Centering a Line

Centering a line in WordPerfect is much simpler than centering a line on an ordinary typewriter. The command **[Shift] + [F6]** allows you to center a line quickly and easily.

In the following exercise, you will add the title WORDPERFECT 5.1 to the third line of the document. With the cursor at the far left of the third line,

1. . . . .Press **[Shift]+[F6]** to start the centering process.
2. . . . .Type **WORDPERFECT 5.1** and press **[Enter]**
Striking the [Enter] key stops the centering process.

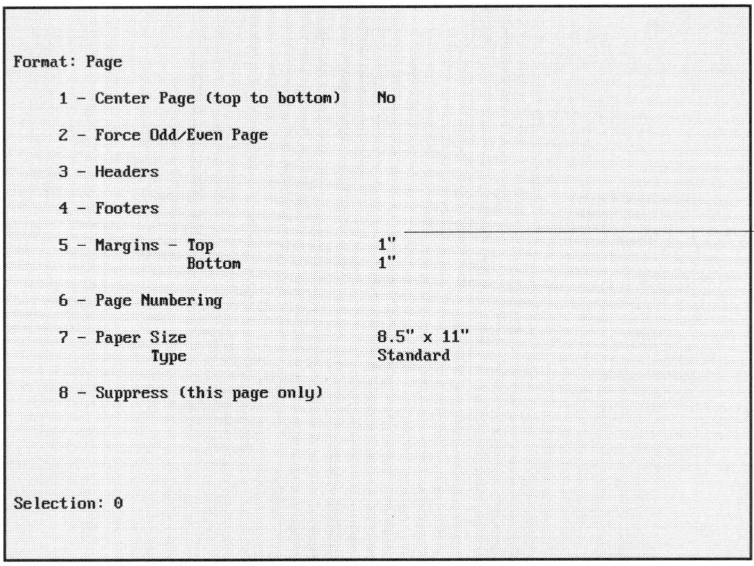

Figure 2-4: *Page Formatting Options & Settings*

Using the Reveal Codes Command

When you use many of the commands in WordPerfect, such as the command for centering a line, the computer automatically inserts codes within the document. Under normal circumstances, these codes do not appear on the screen. However, you can examine these codes by pressing the Reveal Codes **[Alt]+[F3]** keys. If you have a 101 keyboard, you can press the **[F11]** key. The computer will split the screen horizontally. The normal text will appear in the top half of the screen. The bottom half will show the same text but with appropriate codes. Knowing how to use and manipulate the codes is very important.

1.....Press **[Alt]+[F3]** once.
You will see the codes on the split screen. To leave the Reveal Codes feature,

2.....Press **[Alt]+[F3]** a second time.

One of the codes you might see is the **H**ard **R**eturn [HRt] code, which appears when you press the [Enter] key. If you accidentally hit the [Enter] key in Lesson 1 instead of letting the word-wrap feature begin new lines, you can now correct that error. Position the cursor in the lower screen on the **H**ard **R**eturn [HRt] code and press [Delete]. The Hard Return code should only occur at the end of paragraphs and at the beginning of blank lines. The **S**oft **R**eturn [SRt] code at the end of each line indicates the word-wrap feature.

Look at the code used to center the title. When you place the lower-screen cursor on the code and strike the [Delete] key, you will erase that command. You can do the same thing to any character in the text.

Changing Left- and Right-Hand Margins

WordPerfect automatically sets the left- and right-hand margins in a document at one inch in from the left and right sides of the paper. Any margin changes take effect at the position of the cursor. To change the margins for the entire document,

1. ....Press **[Home] [Home] [↑]** to position the cursor at the top of the document.
2. ....Press **[Shift]+[F8]** to select from the Format screen as shown in Figure 2-5.

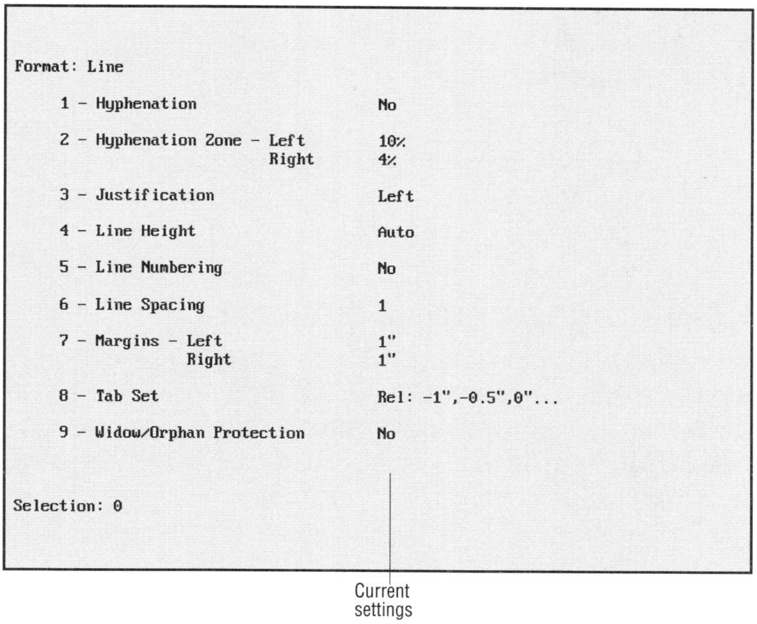

Figure 2-5:
Line Formatting Options & Settings

3. ....Press **1** to select the Line format.
4. ....Press **7** to select the Margin option.

To change the left margin to 2.0 inches from the left edge and the right margin to 1.5 inches from the right edge,

5. ....Type **2** and press **[Enter]** for the new left-hand margin.
6. ....Type **1.5** and press **[Enter]** for the new right-hand margin.
7. ....Press **[Enter] [Enter]** to return to the document.
8. ....Press **[↓]** to go to the bottom of the document.

The document reformats itself according to the new margin settings beginning at the point where the margin code occurs within the document. You can change the margins at any point in the document.

Changing the Top and Bottom Margins

For an 8-1/2-by-11 inch page WordPerfect specifies a top margin of one inch. The normal vertical spacing is 6 lines of text to the inch. Each page contains 66 lines, 54 of which are for text, including headers and footers. You can change the top and bottom margins by using the **[Shift]+[F8]** keys. To set a top margin of one and a half inches for a page,

1.....Press **[Home] [Home] [↑]** to go to the top of the document.
2.....Press **[Shift]+[F8]**, **2** to select the Page Format menu.
3.....Press **5** to select Margins—Top and Bottom.
4.....Type **1.5** and press **[Enter]** to specify the number of inches, here 1.5, from the top of the page.
5.....Press **[Enter]** to keep the 1-inch bottom margin.
6.....Press **[Enter] [Enter]** to return to the document in memory.

Unless you changed the top margin setting at the beginning of the page, only the succeeding pages will have a top margin of 1.5 inches. To change the bottom margin setting, you must specify the new setting before you reach the previously-set margin.

Changing the Line Justification

The Line Justification command allows you to push the lines in the document to the far left, to the far right, to the center of the page, and to stretch them from the left margin to the right margin. No other single command gives you as much power to affect your document's appearance as does the Line Justification command.

In this exercise, you will change the Line Justification for your document to left-justified.

1.....Press **[Home] [Home] [Home] [↑]** to position the cursor at the top of the screen before any hidden codes.
2.....Press **[Shift]+[F8]** to retrieve the Format menu shown in Figure 2-3.
3.....Press **1** to select the Line format menu shown in Figure 2-6.
4.....Press **3** to select Justification.
   The following menu will appear at the bottom of the screen:
   Justification: 1 Left; **2 C**enter; **3 R**ight; **4 F**ull: **0**

5.....Press **1** to change the justification of the current document to left justification.
6.....Press **[Enter] [Enter]** to return to the document in Edit mode.

The document on the screen will not look any different than it did before you changed it to left justification. To see what it will look like when printed, use the View option of the Print command. Press **[F7]** to return to the document.

Print the document.

Using the Reveal Codes command, locate and erase the justification code, **[Just: Left]**. Repeat the line justification procedure but select the full justification option **(4)**. The full justification option will cause the lines to be both right- and left-justified. The document margins will have no ragged edges. Use the View option to see what the document will look like when printed.

Print the document and compare it to the left-justified document.

If you choose a right justification, your document will have a ragged left margin unless all lines contain the same number of characters. Each line will end at the right margin.

Erase the full justification codes. Repeat the line justification procedure and select center justification using the steps given above. Move the cursor to the end of the document. This time you do not need to use the View option to see the results of the justification selection.

Do not save the document, but clear the screen.

Changing the Line Height

Line height refers to the amount of vertical space within which a line is printed. Within the normal line spacing of 6 lines to the inch, the line height is .167 inches. If you change the line height to .333 inches, there will be 3 lines to the inch.

In this exercise, you will change the line height in your document to .2 inches.

Retrieve your LESSON1 file.

1.....Press **[Home] [Home] [Home] [↑]** to position the cursor at the top of the screen before any hidden codes.
2.....Press **[Shift]+[F8]** to retrieve the Format menu shown in Figure 2-3.
3.....Press **1** to select the Line format menu shown in Figure 2-5.
4.....Press **4** to select the Line Height.

The menu choices on the status line are:

(1) **Auto**, which means the WordPerfect program will automatically determine the height of the line based upon the size pitch for the font involved.

(2) **Fixed**, which means the user can determine the height of the line regardless of the pitch size.

To specify a line height of .2 inches,

5.....Press **2**
6.....Type **.2** and press **[Enter]**

To return to your document,

7.....Press **[Enter] [Enter]**.

The status line indicator that shows the distance of the line from the top of the page changes by .2 of an inch each time the cursor passes a line. Any time you invoke the Line Height command, the command will affect only the part of the document that comes after the point at which you issued the command.

Print the document. Clear the screen without saving the file.

NOTE: If the printout has an extra line or two in the body of the text, your printer probably cannot handle the .2 line height.

Changing the Line Spacing

WordPerfect's normal line spacing is single spacing. If you want to change to double spacing or some other line spacing, use the **[Shift]+[F8]** keys.

For the following exercise, retrieve your LESSON1 file. To set the line spacing for the entire document to line and a half,

1. ....Press **[Home] [Home] [↑]** to position the cursor at the top of the document.
2. ....Press **[Shift]+[F8]** to retrieve the Format menu.
3. ....Press **1** to select the Line format menu.
4. ....Press **6** to select the Line Spacing option.
5. ....Type **1.5** and press **[Enter]** to select one and a half lines as the line spacing.
6. ....Press **[Enter] [Enter]** to return to the document. Your spacing change appears in the document.

Clear the screen without saving the margin and spacing changes.

Creating Underlined Text

When you create a document, you may find that you want to emphasize a word or phrase. One way to do that is to underline that word or phrase by using the Underline feature **[F8]**. Underlining is a two-step procedure that involves starting the feature and stopping it when finished.

Retrieve your LESSON1 file and insert two blank lines between paragraphs one and two. Position the cursor on the middle blank line.

To underline automatically while typing the phrase "Fundamentals and Features,"

1. ....Press **[F8]** to start the underlining feature.
2. ....Type **Fundamentals and Features**
3. ....Press **[F8]** to stop the underlining feature.

Pressing the [F8] key a second time tells the word processor when to stop underlining.

Creating Bold Text

Another method of emphasizing a word or a phrase is to bold the text. You can type bold text anywhere within the document. You activate the Bold feature by using the **[F6]** key.

Insert two more blank lines between paragraphs two and three of your document. Position the cursor on the middle blank line.

To bold automatically while typing the phrase "Advanced Features,"

1. . . . .Press **[F6]** to start the bold feature.
2. . . . .Type **Advanced Features**
3. . . . .Press **[F6]** to stop the bold feature.

Do not save the current document. Clear the screen to do the following practice exercises.

General Exercises

If you have exited WordPerfect, load it and retrieve your LESSON1 file.

1. Change the left- and right-hand margins to 2 inches for the entire document.
2. Change the line height in the second paragraph only to .2 inches. Be sure to set the line height back to .167 inches at the start of the third paragraph.
3. Double-space the last paragraph only. Print the file with all of the above changes.
4. Clear the screen without saving the document and retrieve your LESSON1 file again.
   A. Insert four blank lines at the top of the document.
   B. On the first blank line, type your name at the left.
   C. Beginning on the second blank line, type in capital letters, center, and bold the following title:

      USING WORDPERFECT 5.1

   D. Insert two blank lines between paragraphs one and two.
   E. At the left margin on the middle blank line between paragraphs one and two, type, underline and bold the following phrase:

      <u>Fundamental Principles and Features</u>

   F. Save the file as LESSON2.
   G. Print the document.
5. Using the Help command, find the combination of keys to press to
   A. Count words in a document.

B. Find out what the Beep and Backup options are.

C. Put a password on a document.

D. Convert a 5.1 document to 5.0 or 4.2.

E. If you intend to go on to another set of exercises, clear the screen without saving the above changes. If not, exit WordPerfect without saving the above changes.

Course-Specific Exercises

Group A Accounting

Load WordPerfect if necessary and retrieve your ACCTG.ONE file.

1. Change the left margin to 2 inches and the right margin to 2.5 inches.
2. Change the line height to .25 inches.
3. Double-space the second paragraph only.
4. Clear the screen and retrieve the ACCTG.ONE file again.

   A. Insert four blank lines at the top of the document.

   B. On the first blank line, type your name at the left.

   C. Beginning on the third blank line, type in capital letters, center, and bold the following title:

   FUNCTION OF ACCOUNTING

   D. Insert two blank lines between paragraphs one and two.

   E. At the left margin on the middle blank line between paragraphs two and three, type, underline and bold the following title and enter the paragraph:

   Managerial Accounting

   Managerial accounting is similar to financial accounting except that it is used mainly for gathering information to assist management in decision making. Managerial accounting is not controlled by government regulations. It enables the firm to follow actual cash flows and production costs without the hinderance of tax laws and regulations.

   F. Save the file as ACCTG.TWO.

   G. Print the document.

5. Using the Help command, find the key combinations to

   A. Cancel all print jobs.

   B. Select the base font.

   C. Release the left margin.

6. If you intend to go on to another set of exercises, clear the screen without saving the above changes. If not, exit WordPerfect without saving the above document.

Group B Marketing

Load WordPerfect if necessary. Retrieve your MARKTING.ONE file.

1. Change the left margin to 1.75 inches and the right margin to 1.25 inches.
2. Change the line height to .14 inches.
3. Double-space the first paragraph only.
4. Clear the screen and retrieve the MARKTING.ONE file again.
   A. Insert four blank lines at the top of the document.
   B. On the second blank line, enter your name on the center of the line.
   C. On the first blank line, type in capital letters, center, and bold the following title:

      MARKETING MIX

   D. Insert two blank lines between paragraphs one and two.
   E. At the left margin on the middle blank line between paragraphs two and three, type, underline and bold the following title and enter the paragraph:

      <u>A Marketing Problem</u>

      Management must watch out for marketing myopia, one possible problem that can beset a company. This myopia exists when management fails to recognize the scope of its business. When management is product-oriented rather than customer-oriented, a company's growth may be endangered. Management must broadly define its business goals, and orient these goals toward consumer needs.

   F. Save the file as MARKTING.TWO.
   G. Print the document.
5. Using the Help command, find the key combinations to
   A. Switch documents on the screen.
   B. Set a timed document backup.
   C. Encrypt a document.
   D. Delete a file on disk.
6. If you intend to go on to another set of exercises, clear the screen without saving the above changes. If not, exit WordPerfect without saving the above changes.

Group C Finance

Load WordPerfect if necessary. Retrieve your FINANCE.ONE file.

1. Change the left margin to 1.25 inches and the right margin to 1.4 inches.
2. Change the line height to .12 inches.
3. Double-space the last paragraph only.
4. Clear the screen and retrieve the FINANCE.ONE file again.
   A. Insert four blank lines at the top of the document.

B. On the second blank line, enter your name on the center of the line.

C. On the first blank line, type in capital letters, center, and bold the following title:

FUNCTION OF FINANCIAL MANAGEMENT

D. Insert two blank lines between paragraphs one and two.

E. At the left margin on the middle blank line between paragraphs two and three, type, underline and bold the following title and enter the paragraph:

Social Responsibility

Is maximizing stock prices good or bad for society? In general, maximizing stock prices is good. It requires efficient use of resources, and leads to new technology, new products and new jobs. Sales are necessary for profits. Efficient service, adequate stocks of merchandise, and well located businesses create sales and, in turn, these things directly benefit society.

F. Save the file as FINANCE.TWO.

G. Print the document.

5. Using the Help command, find the key combinations to
   - A. Use fine print.
   - B. Ascertain hyphenation rules.
   - C. Do line numbering.
   - D. Underline spaces and tabs.
6. If you intend to go on to another set of exercises, clear the screen without saving the above changes. If not, exit WordPerfect without saving the above changes.

Group D Production

Load WordPerfect if necessary. Retrieve your PRODUCT.ONE file.

1. Change the left margin to 2.25 inches and the right margin to 2.4 inches.
2. Change the line height to .18 inches.
3. Change the last paragraph to line-and-a-half spacing.
4. Clear the screen and retrieve the PRODUCT.ONE file again.
   - A. Insert four blank lines at the top of the document.
   - B. On the second blank line, enter your name on the center of the line.
   - C. On the first blank line, type in capital letters, center, and bold the following title:

IMPLEMENTING JIT IN A BUILD-TO-ORDER ENVIRONMENT

D. Insert two blank lines between paragraphs one and two.

E. At the left margin on the middle blank line between paragraphs one and two, type, underline and bold the following title.

JIT Defined

F. Save the file as PRODUCT.TWO.

G. Print the document.

5. Using the Help command, find the key combinations to

   A. Change font.

   B. Retrieve a file.

   C. Justifying text.

   D. Set the page length.

6. Exit WordPerfect without saving the above changes.

3

Blocking

The objectives of this lesson are to

- Reposition text within a document
- Delete a block of text
- Restore deleted text
- Copy text to other positions in a document
- Bold, underline, center, and change the case of existing text

Moving and Removing Text

The Block function, which uses the command **[Alt]+[F4]**, or the **[F12]** key on the 101 keyboard, is a powerful tool in WordPerfect. The Block function allows you to move, copy, search, protect, replace, flush right, delete, change case, and append text. Some other uses of the Block function allow you to: save, print, center, spell, change the font, underline, and bold existing text. The Block command will precede all of the functions performed in this lesson.

Moving Text

In this lesson, you will use a file, LETTER, that is on the student data disk. The student data disk contains several files that you will use over the course of this tutorial.

Load WordPerfect and retrieve the LETTER file from the student data disk. When you examine the LETTER file, shown in Figure 3-1, you will see that the first two paragraphs are in the wrong sequence.

To move them to their correct sequence, position the cursor on the "O" of "Our" in the first paragraph.

1.....Press **[Alt]+[F4]** or **[F12]**

The following blinking message will appear at the left edge of the status line:

```
Ms. Alice Heidt
100 Battalion Blvd.
Newburgh, NY  10996-1797

Dear Ms. Heidt:

Our records show your phone number to be 345-5432.  If this has
changed, please inform us immediately by calling this toll-free
number:  1-(800) 897-3777.

Congratulations!  You are a winner in the Lott-a-America
Sweepstakes and are soon to be the recipient of a check for
$5,000,000.00 and an additional bonus of a Lamborghini Countach.

The deadline for claiming your prizes is one year from the date of
this letter.  An Internal Revenue Agent will have to be present
when you claim your prizes.

As the winner of the Lott-a-America Sweepstakes, your name is
public information and cannot be withheld from the press.  If you
wish, you can have an attorney claim the prizes in your behalf to
avoid the Television and Press.

Please keep this form for your records.
A:\LETTER                                      Doc 2 Pg 1 Ln 1" Pos 1"
```

Figure 3-1: *Letter File*

Block on

Move the cursor down four lines to highlight the entire paragraph and the line below it. Note that you have highlighted four lines. Subsequent commands will affect this highlighted material. If you highlighted too many lines, reverse the direction of the cursor movement.

You can block and move any string of characters. You can now proceed with the Move — cut and paste — function.

2. . . . .Press **[Ctrl]+[F4]**

You will see the following menu on the status line:

Move: 1 Block; **2** Tabular **C**olumn; **3 R**ectangle: **0**

3. . . . .Press **1** or **B**

Note that in the above menu, the **B** of Block, **C** of tabular Column and **R** of Rectangle are as bright as the numbers preceding them. Any time a menu has another character as bright as the numeric selection, pressing the character will achieve the same result as pressing the numeral.

The following menu will appear on the status line:

1 Move: **2 C**opy; **3 D**elete; **4 A**ppend: **0**

4. . . . .Press **1** to cut the copy from the text.

The entire highlighted paragraph disappears.

Position the cursor at the beginning of the new location for the cut paragraph, on the "P" of "Please."

5. . . . .Press **[Enter]**

The cut paragraph has reappeared (pasted) in its new position.

Use the editing keys [Enter] and/or [Delete] if the paragraphs are not properly positioned within the letter.

Deleting Text

You can delete any amount of text by blocking the unwanted material and striking the **[Delete]** key.

To delete the third and fourth paragraphs of the LETTER file, position the cursor on the "A" of "As" at the beginning of the third paragraph.

1.....Press **[Alt]+[F4]** or **[F12]**
Move the cursor down eight lines.
2.....Press **[Delete]**
In response to the prompt question:

Delete Block? No (**Y**es)

3.....Press **Y** to delete the previously highlighted (blocked) material of the letter as shown in Figure 3-2. You can use these commands to block and delete any string of characters.

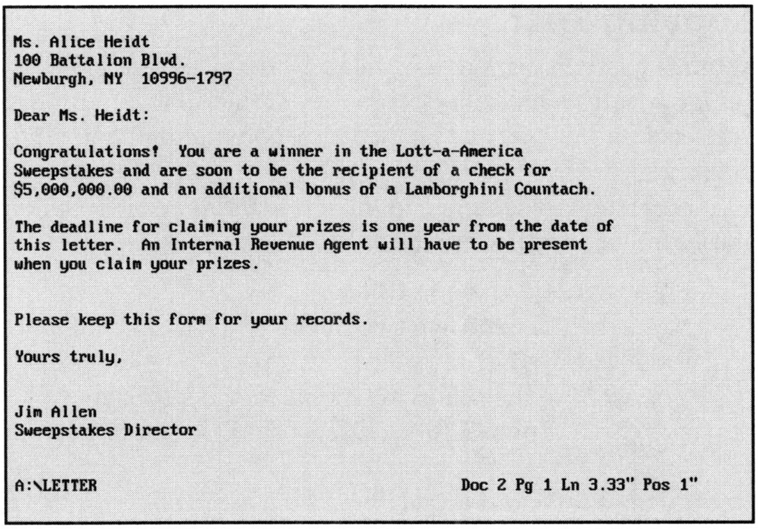

```
Ms. Alice Heidt
100 Battalion Blvd.
Newburgh, NY  10996-1797

Dear Ms. Heidt:

Congratulations!  You are a winner in the Lott-a-America
Sweepstakes and are soon to be the recipient of a check for
$5,000,000.00 and an additional bonus of a Lamborghini Countach.

The deadline for claiming your prizes is one year from the date of
this letter.  An Internal Revenue Agent will have to be present
when you claim your prizes.


Please keep this form for your records.

Yours truly,


Jim Allen
Sweepstakes Director

A:\LETTER                                  Doc 2 Pg 1 Ln 3.33" Pos 1"
```

Figure 3-2:
Third & Fourth Paragraphs Deleted

Restoring Text

In Lesson 2, you learned that the Cancel key [F1] will stop any function that you have started but do not want to complete. In this lesson, you will use the Cancel key to restore text which was deleted. WordPerfect retains in memory the last three deletions of text. You can restore this deleted text to the document by using **[F1]** at the position of the cursor.

To restore the third and fourth paragraphs which you deleted from the letter, position the cursor where you want the material to be placed, on the "P" of "Please."

1.....Press **[F1]**
The previously deleted material is now highlighted. The following menu appears on the status line:
Undelete: 1 Restore; **2 P**revious Deletion: **0**

2.....Press **1**
You have restored both the third and fourth paragraphs to the document.

The Restore feature in WordPerfect allows you to change your mind after you have discarded material. The first time you accidentally delete vital material, you will begin to appreciate the usefulness of this feature!

Do keep in mind, however, that the program only stores the last three changes to the text. If you make a change, such as a deletion, and then make more than two other changes, the change will no longer be accessible for restoration.

Copying Text

At times you will want to use the same text in several places within a document or even in different documents. Rather than enter the same material over each time, you can use the Copy command **[Ctrl] + [F4], 1**, **2** to avoid the drudgery of repetitious typing.

To copy the last sentence in the letter and place it between each paragraph, move the cursor to the "P" of "Please."

1.....Press **[Alt]+[F4]** or **[F12]**
Move the cursor down two lines.
2.....Press **[Ctrl]+[F4]**
You will see the following menu on the status line:
Move: 1 Block; **2** Tabular **C**olumn; **3 R**ectangle: **0**

3.....Press **1** to select Block.
From the new menu on the status line,
1 Move; **2 C**opy; **3 D**elete; **4 A**ppend: 0

4.....Press **2** and the highlight is removed.
The following message appears on the status line:
Move cursor; press **[Enter]** to retrieve.

Move the cursor to the "O" of "Our" in the fourth paragraph.
5.....Press **[Enter]**

The copied text now appears between paragraphs three and four while the original remains after paragraph four, as shown in Figure 3-3. You can continue to copy the same text by positioning the cursor on the "A" of "As" in paragraph 3.

```
Newburgh, NY  10996-1797

Dear Ms. Heidt:

Congratulations!  You are a winner in the Lott-a-America
Sweepstakes and are soon to be the recipient of a check for
$5,000,000.00 and an additional bonus of a Lamborghini Countach.

The deadline for claiming your prizes is one year from the date of
this letter.  An Internal Revenue Agent will have to be present
when you claim your prizes.

As the winner of the Lott-a-America Sweepstakes, your name is
public information and cannot be withheld from the press.  If you
wish, you can have an attorney claim the prizes in your behalf to
avoid the Television and Press.

Please keep this form for your records.

Our records show your phone number to be 345-5432.  If this has
changed, please inform us immediately by calling this toll-free
number:  1-(800) 897-3777.

Please keep this form for your records.
A:\LETTER                                   Doc 2 Pg 1 Ln 4.17" Pos 1"
```

Copied text

Figure 3-3: *Result of Copy Command*

6.....Press **[Ctrl]+[F4]**
The following menu will appear on the status line:
Move: 1 Sentence; **2 P**aragraph; **3 P**a**g**e; **4 R**etrieve: **0**

7.....Press **4**
From the next menu on the status line,
Retrieve: 1 Block; **2** Tabular **C**olumn; **3 R**ectangle: **0**

8.....Press **1**
This procedure places a block of material that has been previously cut or copied at the point of the cursor as shown in Figure 3-4.

Clear the screen. Do not save the file.

Bolding Existing Text

After you have written a section of text, you might want to make it stand out by bolding it. You could erase all of the text and retype it after invoking the bold function. However, you can avoid retyping the section by blocking the affected material and then invoking the function **[F6]**.

Retrieve the LETTER file. To bold the last sentence in the letter, position the cursor at the "P" of "Please" and

1.....Press **[Alt]+[F4]** or **[F12]**
Move the cursor down one line.

```
Newburgh, NY  10996-1797

Dear Ms. Heidt:

Congratulations!  You are a winner in the Lott-a-America
Sweepstakes and are soon to be the recipient of a check for
$5,000,000.00 and an additional bonus of a Lamborghini Countach.

The deadline for claiming your prizes is one year from the date of
this letter.  An Internal Revenue Agent will have to be present
when you claim your prizes.

Please keep this form for your records.

As the winner of the Lott-a-America Sweepstakes, your name is
public information and cannot be withheld from the press.  If you
wish, you can have an attorney claim the prizes in your behalf to
avoid the Television and Press.

Please keep this form for your records.

Our records show your phone number to be 345-5432.  If this has
changed, please inform us immediately by calling this toll-free
number:  1-(800) 897-3777.
A:\LETTER                                   Doc 2 Pg 1 Ln 3.33" Pos 1"
```

Second copy of same text

Figure 3-4: *Repeated Text Copy*

2. . . . .Press **[F6]**

Note that this procedure has changed the text's appearance on the screen. The text is bolded, you can check for the hidden Bold code by invoking the Reveal Codes features, **[Alt]** + **[F3]**.

Underlining Existing Text

You can also use the Block function to underline existing text by choosing the **[F8]** key instead of [F6]. To underline the phrase "Lamborghini Countach" in the first paragraph, position the cursor on the "L" of "Lamborghini."

1. . . . .Press **[Alt]+[F4]** or **[F12]**
   Move the cursor to the end of the phrase.
2. . . . .Press **[F8]**

Use the Reveal Codes feature to verify that you have underlined "Lamborghini Countach."

Centering Existing Text

You may have a left-justified heading that you would now like to center. Rather than retyping the heading, use the blocking and centering feature.

To center the last sentence in the letter, position the cursor on the "P" of "Please."

1. . . . .Press **[Alt]+[F4]** or **[F12]**
   Move the cursor down one line.
2. . . . .Press **[Shift]+[F6]**
   The following prompt appears:

[Just:Center]? No (**Y**es)

3. . . . .Press **Y** and the blocked material will be centered.

Changing Case

Another way of emphasizing a piece of text is putting it in capital letters. To capitalize letters in existing text, use the Switch Case command **[Shift] + [F3]**. To change the last sentence of the letter to caps, position the cursor at the "P" of "Please."

1. . . . .Press **[Alt]+[F4]** or **[F12]**
   Move the cursor down one line.
2. . . . .Press **[Shift]+[F3]**
   From the menu that appears,
3. . . . .Press **1** to select uppercase.

The text is now in caps. You can change any amount of blocked text to all uppercase or lowercase letters.

Save the current file as LESSON3. Clear the screen and do the following practice exercises.

General Exercises

Retrieve your LESSON3 file.

1. Change the entire letter to uppercase.
2. Bold and underline the phrase "$5,000,000.00."
3. Center and bold the fourth paragraph.
4. Delete the second paragraph.
5. Restore the deleted paragraph one line above the closing.
6. Print the document with the above changes.
7. Save the document as PRAC3. If you intend to go on to another set of exercises, clear the screen. If not, exit WordPerfect.

Course-Specific Exercises

Group A Accounting

Load WordPerfect and retrieve your ACCTG.ONE file.

1. Change the entire document to uppercase.
2. Move the sentence in the third paragraph that starts "The accounting . . ." to the end of the first paragraph.
3. Bold and underline "planning, control, and evaluation" in the third paragraph.
4. Bold the last paragraph.
5. Delete the second paragraph.
6. Restore the deleted paragraph one line above the first paragraph.
7. Print the document with the above changes.

8. Save the document as PRACTICE.ACT. If you intend to go on to another set of exercises, clear the screen. If not, exit WordPerfect.

Group B Marketing

Load WordPerfect if necessary. Retrieve your MARKTING.ONE file.

1. Change the second paragraph to uppercase.
2. Move the last sentence in the second paragraph to the end of the first paragraph.
3. Bold and underline the phrase "(1) price ... (4) place" in the third paragraph.
4. Bold the second paragraph.
5. Delete the first paragraph.
6. Restore the deleted paragraph one line below the last paragraph.
7. Print the document with the above changes.
8. Save the document as PRACTICE.MKT. If you intend to go on to another set of exercises, clear the screen. If not, exit WordPerfect.

Group C Finance

Load WordPerfect if necessary. Retrieve your FINANCE.ONE file.

1. Change the entire document to lowercase.
2. Move the first sentence in the third paragraph to the end of the second paragraph.
3. Bold and underline the last sentence in the last paragraph.
4. Bold the first paragraph.
5. Delete the second paragraph.
6. Restore the deleted paragraph one line above the first paragraph.
7. Print the document with the above changes.
8. Save the document as PRACTICE.FIN. If you intend to go on to another set of exercises, clear the screen. If not, exit WordPerfect.

Group D Production

Load WordPerfect if necessary. Retrieve your PRODUCT.ONE file.

1. Change the last paragraph to uppercase.
2. Move the last sentence in the second paragraph to the end of the third paragraph.
3. Bold and underline "JIT."
4. Bold the numbered items in the last sentence of the first paragraph.
5. Delete the second paragraph.
6. Restore the deleted paragraph one line below the last paragraph.
7. Print the document with the above changes.
8. Save the document as PRACTICE.PRT and exit WordPerfect.

4

Pagination and Indention

The objectives of this lesson are to

- Create automatic page numbering
- Create headers and footers
- Set tab stops
- Set paragraph indents
- Set indents on left and right margins

Selecting the Page Number and Position

When you invoke the page numbering command **[Shift]+[F8], 2, 6,** WordPerfect will automatically number each page of your document in consecutive order. You can select the number's position on the page and even the pages to be numbered. In addition, you can use either arabic or roman numerals. Roman numerals can be either uppercase or lowercase.

Retrieve your LESSON1 file. To put a page number in the top right corner of the page, move the cursor to the top of the document.

1.....Press **[Shift]+[F8], 2** to select Format: Page.
2.....Press **6** to select Page Numbering.
3.....Press **1** to select New Page Number.

The prompt will ask you to type in a number with which to begin numbering the pages of the document. You can type in an arabic numeral or a roman numeral, for example, 1 or I or i. In this exercise, type i and then

4.....Press **[Enter]** to tell the computer the beginning page number and return to the Page Numbering Format screen.
5.....Press **4** to select Page Numbering Position.
6.....Press **3** to choose Upper Right of every page.
7.....Press **[F7]** to return to the document.

The page number will not appear on your screen. However, it will appear when you print the document. To check that the page-numbering option does exist in the document without printing, use the Reveal Codes command **[Alt]+[F3]** and examine the first line. By default, WordPerfect will automatically choose arabic numerals and start with the number 1 unless you specify roman numerals and/or a different beginning page number.

Creating Headers and Footers

A header is a line of standard text that appears at the top of each page, and a footer is a line that appears at the bottom. Headers and footers are used in books, reports and reference works to insert titles, labels and page numbers. You can place them at the top or bottom of every page, every odd-numbered page, or every even-numbered page by invoking the command **[Shift]+[F8], 2, 3**.

Like page numbers, headers and footers are invisible on the editing screen and only appear when printed, or when you use the Reveal Codes command to verify that they have been correctly added.

To place a header and/or footer on every page of your document, move the cursor to the beginning of the top line of the first page of the document.

1.....Press **[Shift]+[F8], 2** to select Format: Page.
2.....Press **3** to select Headers.
The menu will offer you two possible headers:
1 Header **A**; **2** Header **B**: 0

3.....Press **1** to select Header A.
4.....Press **2** to put header A on every page.
Type the following heading:
WordPerfect Version 5.1 Features

When you enter the header, you can use any combination of formatting features such as bolding, underlining and centering. You can also include page numbering.

5.....Press **[F7] [F7]** to return to the document.

You can create a footer the same way you create a header, except that you would choose the footer option instead of the header option from the page format menu.

To include automatic page numbering within the header or footer, use the command **[Ctrl]+[B]**.

To create a centered, automatically numbered footer that will say "Page - n" —where "n" is the page number—on every page,

1.....Press **[Shift]+[F8], 2, 4, 1, 2**
2.....Press **[Shift]+[F6]**
3.....Type **Page -** this is the text part of the footer.
4.....Press **[Ctrl]+[B]** to insert the code to create the automatic page numbering.

5. . . . .Press **[F7]** twice to return to the document.

Save the file as LESSON4 and clear the screen.

Setting Indention

WordPerfect has three different kinds of indent keys: 1) tab, 2) left indent, and 3) left/right indent. The tab indent is a command that takes effect immediately and then stops. The other two types of indents remain in effect until the [Enter] key is pressed.

Using the Tab Indent

Clear the screen and retrieve your LESSON4 file. Position the cursor at the top of the document.

1. . . . .Press **[Tab]**

Note that the top line moved five spaces to the right, which is where the next tab stop is located. Use the Reveal Codes command to examine the hidden code [Tab] for the tab command.

The tab command indents the margin for just the one line in which you use it. If you want to change the indentation for more than one line, use the left indent or left/right indent command.

Using the Left Indent

When you want to change temporarily the left-hand margin to the next tab stop position, use the Indent key **[F4]**. Unlike the tab indent, this change will remain in effect until you press the [Enter] key.

Position the cursor at the beginning of the second paragraph.

1. . . . .Press **[F4]**
2. . . . .Move the cursor to the beginning of the third paragraph. The entire second paragraph has been reformatted as shown in Figure 4-1.

Use the Reveal Codes command to examine this command code, which appears as [Indent].

Using the Left/Right Indent

The third indent function temporarily indents both the left- and right-hand margins equally to the next tab stop. To use the left/right indent, press **[Shift]+[F4]**. Pressing [Enter] will stop the left/right indent.

To indent both the right and left margins, position the cursor at the beginning of the third paragraph.

1. . . . .Press **[Shift]+[F4] [PgDn]**

Tab

Left indent

```
     WordPerfect 5.1 is one of the most powerful and comprehensive
word processing programs available.  It is fast, efficient, and a
genuine pleasure to use.  However, the program is better known for
an abundance of helpful features and the fact that WordPerfect
Corporation keeps making each version more proficient.

     WordPerfect 5.1 has all of the fundamental word processing
     functions available, such as automatic word wrap, which
     creates a new line when the cursor reaches the right margin
     and moves the cursor down to the new line.  It also does
     automatic rewrite, which automatically reformats your
     paragraphs after any editing changes, such as adding or
     deleting text through keyboard entry or using search and
     replace commands to locate and/or change a word or phrase.

WordPerfect 5.1 has abilities which extend way beyond the basics to
include special features some of which are a pull-down menu, a
spelling checker, a thesaurus, automatic footnotes and endnotes,
newspaper columns, and alphabetical and numeric sorting.
Additionally, it is possible to create graphics, spreadsheets,
macros, line drawings, equations, and mathematical functions to
perform addition, subtraction, multiplication, division and
averaging.

A:\LESSON4                                   Doc 1 Pg 1 Ln 3.83" Pos 1"
```

Figure 4-1: *Result of Tab & Left Indent Commands*

Note that the right-hand margin is indented as much as the left-hand margin. (See Figure 4-2.)

Left indent

Right indent

```
genuine pleasure to use.  However, the program is better known for
an abundance of helpful features and the fact that WordPerfect
Corporation keeps making each version more proficient.

     WordPerfect 5.1 has all of the fundamental word processing
     functions available, such as automatic word wrap, which
     creates a new line when the cursor reaches the right margin
     and moves the cursor down to the new line.  It also does
     automatic rewrite, which automatically reformats your
     paragraphs after any editing changes, such as adding or
     deleting text through keyboard entry or using search and
     replace commands to locate and/or change a word or phrase.

     WordPerfect 5.1 has abilities which extend way beyond the
     basics to include special features some of which are a
     pull-down menu, a spelling checker, a thesaurus,
     automatic footnotes and endnotes, newspaper columns, and
     alphabetical and numeric sorting.  Additionally, it is
     possible to create graphics, spreadsheets, macros, line
     drawings, equations, and mathematical functions to
     perform addition, subtraction, multiplication, division
     and averaging.

A:\LESSON4                                   Doc 1 Pg 1 Ln 5.33" Pos 1"
```

Figure 4-2: *Left & Right Indent*

Print the document. Clear the screen without saving the document.

Setting Tab Stops

Every time you create a new document, WordPerfect automatically sets the tab stops for every five columns beginning at column 0 (zero). You can tailor the tab stops to your own needs by using the Format Line function. WordPerfect 5.1 allows you to set the tab stops in either the absolute position or a position relative to the left margin. In the following exercise, you will use the relative tab setting.

You can set tab stops for left and right justification as well as centered. You can also set tab stops to align numeric values on the decimal point and to place dot (.) leaders to the left of a right-justified tab position.

Retrieve LESSON4. Position the cursor at the top of the document.

1.....Press **[Shift]+[F8]** to select Format.

2.....Press **1** to select the Line Format.

3.....Press **8** to select Tab Set. You will see a display of the tab stops, (L) for Left, and the column position of the tab stops, as shown in Figure 4-3.

```
WordPerfect 5.1 is one of the most powerful and comprehensive word
processing programs available.  It is fast, efficient, and a
genuine pleasure to use.  However, the program is better known for
an abundance of helpful features and the fact that WordPerfect
Corporation keeps making each version more proficient.

WordPerfect 5.1 has all of the fundamental word processing
functions available, such as automatic word wrap, which creates a
new line when the cursor reaches the right margin and moves the
cursor down to the new line.  It also does automatic rewrite, which
automatically reformats your paragraphs after any editing changes,
such as adding or deleting text through keyboard entry or using
search and replace commands to locate and/or change a word or
phrase.

WordPerfect 5.1 has abilities which extend way beyond the basics to
include special features some of which are a pull-down menu, a
spelling checker, a thesaurus, automatic footnotes and endnotes,
newspaper columns, and alphabetical and numeric sorting.
Additionally, it is possible to create graphics, spreadsheets,
L....L....L....L....L....L....L....L....L....L....L....L....L....L....L....L...   Tab Ruler
!    ^    !    ^    !    ^    !    ^    !    ^    !    ^    !    ^    !    ^
0"        +1"       +2"       +3"       +4"       +5"       +6"       +7"
Delete EOL (clear tabs); Enter Number (set tab); Del (clear tab);
Type; Left; Center; Right; Decimal; .= Dot Leader; Press Exit when done.
```

Figure 4-3:
Tab Rules & Initial Tab Settings

4.....Press **[Ctrl]+[End]** to erase all tab stops to the right of the cursor.

WordPerfect gives you two ways to set left-justified tab stops. The first allows you to move the cursor to the column where you want a tab stop and then strike the **L** key. The second allows you to type in the column number you want and then press [Enter].

To set a left-justified tab stop at columns 20 and 30,

5.....Press **T** to select the Tab Type option.

6.....Press **R** to select the relative tab setting.

7.....Move the cursor to column 20 and press **L**. Move the cursor to column 30 and again press **L**.

8.....Press **[F7]** twice to return to the document.

You now have a new set of relative tab stops. To see the effects of a tab [Tab], a left indent [F4], and a left/right indent [Shift]+[F4], position the cursor at the beginning of the first paragraph.

1.....Press **[Tab]**

Position the cursor at the beginning of the second paragraph.

2.....Press **[F4]**

Position the cursor at the beginning of the third paragraph and

3.....Press **[Shift]+[F4]**

Print the document and compare the two printed documents. Notice in what ways they are different.

Clear the screen. Do not save the file.

You can use the tab [Tab] and the left indent key [F4] to create a hanging indention, which indents all of the lines in a paragraph except for the first line. The [Tab] key temporarily changes the left margin to the next left tab stop when you hold the [Shift] key down at the same time.

To create a hanging indention, retrieve your LESSON4 file and position the cursor at the beginning of the document. Clear all tab stops and set new ones at 0, 0.5 and 1.0 inches from the left margin.

1.....Press **[F4] [F4] [Shift]+[Tab] [PgDn]** to create a hanging indentation.

2.....Press **[PgDn]** to realign text.

The right-justified tab stop and the dot leader tab stop are similar. The dot leader tab automatically places dots or periods from the left to the right tab stop.

To create a dot leader, clear all tab stops. In this example, position the cursor at 4.0 inches and press (.). The character on the tab line at that point will be an "R."

Return to the document and type **Gone With the Wind** and press **[Tab]** **1936** and press **[Enter]**

You will see **Gone With the Wind .... 1936**. Note that the line is justified, with the "G" of "Gone" on the left and the last digit of "1936" on the right. If you type additional movie titles and the year of their release, each line will be justified on the left by the first character of the title and on the right by the last digit of the year.

Clear the screen. Do not save the file.

General Exercises

Load WordPerfect if necessary. Retrieve your LESSON4 file.

1. Create the following header:

   <u>Indention Features</u>.

2. Create and center the following footer where n is the page number:

   WORDPERFECT MANUAL - PAGE n.

   Print the file.

3. Create and center a footer as above, but instead of using 1 to number the first page, use this year in roman numerals for the beginning page number. (1991 = MCMXCI, ... , 2000 = MM)
4. Clear all tab stops and set a single tab stop in column 17.
5. Number each paragraph consecutively, placing the numbers at the beginning of the paragraphs and following the numbers with a left indent. Save the file as LESSON4A and print it.
6. Number the paragraphs as above, but use the left/right indent feature instead of the left indent. Save the file as LESSON4B and print it.
7. If you intend to go on to another set of exercises, clear the screen. If not, exit WordPerfect.

Course-Specific Exercises

Group A Accounting

Load WordPerfect if necessary. Retrieve your ACCTG.TWO document.

1. Create and position the following header at the left margin:

   <u>Accounting Specialties</u>

2. Create and center the following footer where "n" is the page number:

   ACCOUNTING PROFESSION - PAGE n.

3. Clear all tab stops. Set new tab stops at 5 and 10 spaces from the left margin. Use the [Tab] key and the Left Indent [F4] key when you enter the following text at the end of the document:

   FINANCIAL STATEMENTS

   Financial statements provide information about the financial condition of a firm. The four statements used for external reporting are

   1. INCOME STATEMENT

      Revenues and expenses are reported in this statement. Income is equal to revenues minus expenses.

   2. BALANCE SHEET

      The balance sheet has two sides which must be in balance. One side lists assets and their totals. The other side of the balance sheet lists liabilities and equity and their totals.

   3. STATEMENT OF RETAINED EARNINGS

      Net income, for the current period, is added to the retained earnings balance from the previous period. The result is an updated retained earnings balance.

   4. STATEMENT OF CASH FLOWS

      This statement reports sources and uses of cash. If sources exceed uses then the firm has a positive cash flow for the period.

   Print the file.

4. Create and center a footer as in Problem 2, but instead of using 1 to number the first page, use this year in roman numerals for the beginning page number. (1991 = MCMXCI, ... , 2000 = MM)
5. Modify the above footer by using the left/right indent feature instead of the left indent.
6. Save the file as PRCTICE4.ACT. If you intend to go on to another set of exercises, clear the screen. If not, exit WordPerfect.

Group B Marketing

Load WordPerfect if necessary. Retrieve your MARKTING.TWO document.

1. Create and position the following header at the right margin:

   <u>Marketing Careers</u>

2. Create and left-justify the following footer where "n" is the page number:

   MARKETING PROFESSION - PAGE n.

3. Clear all tab stops. Set new tab stops at 5, 20, and 23 spaces from the left margin. Use the [Tab] key and the Left Indent [F4] key when you enter the following text at the end of the document:

   Marketing Mix

   The four P's of a marketing mix are

* Product	:	the goods and services that satisfy the consumer's needs
* Price	:	what is given for the product
* Promotion	:	the means of providing information to the consumer
* Place	:	the means of delivering the product to the consumer

   Print the file.

4. Create a footer as in Problem 2, but instead of using 1 to number the first page, use this year in roman numerals for the beginning page number. (1991 = MCMXCI, ... , 2000 = MM)
5. Modify the above footer by using the left/right indent feature instead of the left indent.
6. Save the file as PRCTICE4.MKT. If you intend to go on to another set of exercises, clear the screen. If not, exit WordPerfect.

Group C Finance

Load WordPerfect if necessary. Retrieve your FINANCE.TWO document.

1. Create and position the following header at the left margin:

   <u>Finance Management Occupations</u>

2. Create and right-justify the following footer where "n" is the page number:

   FINANCE PROFESSION - PAGE n - IFMA.

3. Clear all tab stops. Set new tab stops at 5, 8, and 13 spaces from the left margin. Use the [Tab] key and the left indent [F4] key when you enter the following text at the end of the document:

The Interrelated Areas

The three interrelated areas in finance are (1) money and capital markets, (2) investments, and (3) financial management.

* Money and capital markets deal with many topics covered in macroeconomics.
* Investments are the decisions individuals and financial institutions make as they choose securities for their investment portfolios.
* Financial management or business finance deals with decisions within the firm.

Print the file.

4. Create a footer as in Problem 2, but instead of using 1 to number the first page, use this year in roman numerals for the beginning page number. (1991 = MCMXCI, ... , 2000 = MM)
5. Modify the above footer by using the left/right indent feature instead of the left indent.
6. Save the file as PRCTICE4.FIN. If you intend to go on to another set of exercises, clear the screen. If not, exit WordPerfect.

Group D Production

Load WordPerfect if necessary. Retrieve your PRODUCT.TWO document.

1. Create and center the following header:

The Changing Production Discipline

2. Create and center the following footer where "n" is the page number:

PRODUCTION/OPERATIONS MANAGEMENT - PAGE n.

3. Clear all tab stops. Set new tab stops at 5, 10 and 13 spaces from the left margin. Use the [Tab] key and the Left Indent [F4] key when you enter the following text at the end of the document:

People Problems

A number of people problems can arise before and during the implementation of the JIT process:

* MRP will not let us do that
* "Not invented here" syndrome
* Reluctance to find problems
* Management reluctant to turn over day-to-day operation to the employees
* Employees reluctant to work in a team or to perform as a team.

Print the file.

4. Create a footer as in Problem 2, but instead of using 1 to number the first page, use this year in roman numerals for the beginning page number. (1991 = MCMXCI, ... , 2000 = MM)
5. Modify Problem 3 by using the left/right indent feature instead of the left indent. Save the file as PRCTICE4.PRT and exit WordPerfect.

5

Search and Replace

The objectives of this lesson are to

- Locate the next occurrence of text or hidden codes
- Search forward or backward for text or hidden codes
- Search for text and codes and automatically replace them with other text and codes

Using the Search Feature

WordPerfect allows you to search forward or backward through a document to find text. The text you search for is called a **search string**. A search string can be any word or combination of words. You may type the search string all in lowercase letters, because lowercase letters match both lowercase and uppercase letters. Uppercase letters, however, only match uppercase.

Clear the screen and retrieve your LESSON3 file.

Use the Search key **[F2]** for forward searches. A forward search means the search process begins at the cursor position and goes forward toward the end of the file. If the search is successful, the cursor will stop at the end of the string; otherwise, you will see the message * **Not found** * on the status line.

To conduct a forward search,

1.....Press **[F2]**
The search prompt - **Srch:** will appear on the status line.

2.....Type **Heldt**
Do not press the **[Enter]** key after typing Heldt. If you press the **[Enter]** key, the Enter code will become part of the search string.

3.....Press **[F2]** to activate the forward search for Heldt.
When the search locates "Heldt," the cursor will be at the right edge of the word. To activate the forward search again,

4.....Press **[F2]**

Notice that WordPerfect remembers the last search string, "Heldt," and will continue to search for it until you replace it with another search string. To start the search for "Heldt" again,

5. ....Press **[F2]**
   The search locates another instance of "Heldt."
6. ....Repeat steps 4 and 5 until the search locates no more occurrences of the search string. When there are no more occurrences, you will see the * **Not found** * prompt and you may also hear a beep from the computer.

Now perform a backward search from the position of the cursor to locate the last use of "in."

1. ....Press **[Shift]+[F2]**
   At the backward - **Srch** prompt,
2. ....Type **in**
3. ....Press **[Shift]+[F2]** to activate the backward search. You can continue to repeat the backward search command until you see the * **Not found** * prompt.

The cursor will stop on the string "in" when it is part of other words such as "winner," "calling," and "inform." To search for whole words or phrases, isolate the target word or phrase by placing a space before and after it.

The Search function can also find any WordPerfect hidden codes in the document. To search for the underline [UND] code in the first paragraph, position the cursor at the top of the file.

1. ....Press **[F2]**
2. ....Press **[F8]** to activate the underline code.
   You should see the [UND] code displayed after the forward **-Srch** prompt. To start the forward search,
3. ....Press **[F2]**

When the cursor stops, press Reveal Codes and the [UND] code that activates underlining should appear just to the left of the cursor. At this point, you can either edit the text or continue to search for other occurrences of the underline code.

Using the Search and Replace Feature

In addition to searching forward or backward for text, you can replace text with new text. Similarly, by using the command **[Alt] + [F2]**, you can search for any combination of text and hidden codes and replace them with any other combination of text and codes.

In this exercise, you will change the name "Heldt" to "Jones." Position the cursor at the top of the file.

1. ....Press **[Alt]+[F2]**

The prompt **w/Confirm? N**o (**Y**es) will appear on the status line.

2. . . . .Press **Y** and the forward search prompt - **Srch:** will appear on the status line.

3. . . . .Type **Heldt**
To indicate the end of the word, phrase, or hidden code to be located,

4. . . . .Press **[F2]**
The prompt **Replace with:** will appear on the status line.

5. . . . .Type **Jones**

6. . . . .Press **[F2]** to start the search.
Each time the cursor stops on the name "Heldt," press **Y** to change it to Jones.

Setting the confirm option to **Y** when using Replace allows you to make the final decision on each replacement. Use this as a safety feature to make sure that you do not accidentally change a word or phrase, as when replacing a common word such as "in" which can be contained within other words.

Clear the screen without saving the file.

General Exercises

Retrieve the file PRAC5 from your student data disk.

1. Search for all occurrences of the word "extended" and change them to "expanded."
2. Use the Search and Replace command to change all occurrences of the word "Aromax" to "Aromax and Family."
3. Search for all bold commands in the file and delete them.
4. Save the changed document as PRAC6 on your student data disk.
5. Print the file and note the changes.
6. If you intent to go on to another set of exercises, clear the screen. If not, exit WordPerfect.

Course-Specific Exercises

Group A Accounting

Load WordPerfect if necessary. Retrieve your ACCTG.TWO file from the student data disk.

1. Search for all occurrences of the word "decisions" and change them to "judgments."
2. Search for all occurrences of the word "information" and change them to "data."
3. Search for all underline commands in the file and delete them.
4. Save the changed document as PRAC6.ACT on your student data disk.
5. Print your ACCTG.TWO and PRAC6.ACT files and note the changes.
6. If you intend to go on to another set of exercises, clear the screen. If not, exit WordPerfect.

Group B Marketing

Load WordPerfect if necessary. Retrieve your MARKTING.TWO file from the student data disk.

1. Search for all occurrences of the word "product" and change them to "merchandise."
2. Search for all occurrences of the word "marketing" and change them to "marketing management."
3. Search for all [HRt] commands in the file and replace them with [HRt]. (Pressing [Enter] produces [HRt].)
4. Save the changed document as PRAC6.MKT on your student data disk.
5. Print the MARKTING.TWO and PRAC6.MKT files and note the changes.
6. If you intend to go on to another set of exercises, clear the screen. If not, exit WordPerfect.

Group C Finance

Load WordPerfect if necessary. Retrieve your FINANCE.TWO file from the student data disk.

1. Search for all occurrences of the word "plan" and change them to "arrange."
2. Search for all occurrences of the word "new" and change them to "novel and exciting."
3. Search for all [Tab] commands in the file and replace them with the [Indent] code for the left indent command.
4. Save the changed document as PRAC6.FIN on your student data disk.
5. Print the FINANCE.TWO and PRAC6.FIN files and note the changes.
6. If you intend to go on to another set of exercises, clear the screen. If not, exit WordPerfect.

Group D Production

Load WordPerfect if necessary. Retrieve your PRODUCT.TWO file from the student data disk.

1. Search for all occurrences of the string "JIT" and change them to "Just-In-Time."
2. Search for all occurrences of the word "philosophy" and change them to "ideology."
3. Search for every ")" in the file and replace it with "]".
4. Save the changed document as PRAC6.PRT on your student data disk.
5. Print the PRODUCT.TWO and PRAC6.PRT files and note the changes.
6. Exit WordPerfect.

6

File Management

The objectives of this lesson are to

- Use the List Files menu to retrieve, copy, move, rename, and delete files
- Mark files
- Search all files for a word or phrase
- Make a new directory and change directories
- Use the Look option to view files on disk and see and/or use files in other directories

Managing Files

Good file management is essential for effective word processing, yet is often ignored. Careful file management helps you to control and organize your files so that you can always find the file you need quickly and easily.

Retrieving Multiple Files

You already know how to retrieve a document using List Files **[F5]**. But did you realize that you can create a single larger file by retrieving a series of smaller files? For example, you can create a personalized letter by selecting appropriate paragraphs from a file, including opening and closing paragraphs and paragraphs stating the purpose of the letter. You can even insert new material to create the new, larger file.

In this exercise, you will create a new file composed of existing files. Type and center the following line:

WORDPERFECT 5.1

Add two blank lines after the title and prepare to retrieve your LESSON1 file from the student data disk. (Note that the position of the cursor when you retrieve a file is very important. The first line of the retrieved file will appear at the position of the cursor.)

1.....Press **[F5]**
If the prompt says **Dir A:*.***, press **[Enter]**
If the prompt says **C:WP51*.***, type **A:** and press **[Enter]**
Using the arrows for cursor movement, position the highlighted area on the LESSON1 file.

2.....Press **1**
The following prompt appears on the status line:
Retrieve into current document: No (**Y**es)

3.....Press **Y** to retrieve the file into the current document.
Move the cursor to the end of the file, add a blank line and type the paragraph shown in Figure 6-1.

One of the more basic features is the use of the tab key and the indent key. Each of these key's function is designed to do a specific task. The following is a brief explanation of each key's function.

Figure 6-1:
New Paragraph

Add another blank line at the end of the paragraph and retrieve LESSON1 from the student data disk using the List Files command.

You now have two smaller files making up a third file on the screen. You can save this third file just as you would any other file you create. You can incorporate a file into another file at any time.

Clear the screen. Do not save the file.

Copying Documents

You can use the Copy option **8** of List Files **[F5]** to copy the file to another disk, another directory, or to a different file name in the same directory.

To copy a file to a new file name in the same directory,

1.....Press **[F5]**
If the prompt says **Dir A:*.***, press **[Enter]**
If the prompt says **Dir C:\WP51*.***, type **A:** and press **[Enter]**
Position the highlighted area on the LESSON1 file. From the menu at the bottom of the screen

2.....Press **8**
When the following prompt appears on the status line:
Copy this file to:

3. . . . .Type **TEST1** and press **[Enter]** to copy this file to another file named TEST1.

You have just created a second copy of LESSON1 called TEST1. At this moment TEST1 does not appear on the screen.

To verify that you have created the TEST1 file, exit the List Files screen.

1. . . . .Press **[Space]**
2. . . . .Press **[F5]**

If the prompt says **Dir A:*.***, press **[Enter]**

If the prompt says **Dir C:\WP51*.***, type **A:** and press **[Enter]**

The TEST1 file should appear in the list of files which will look some-

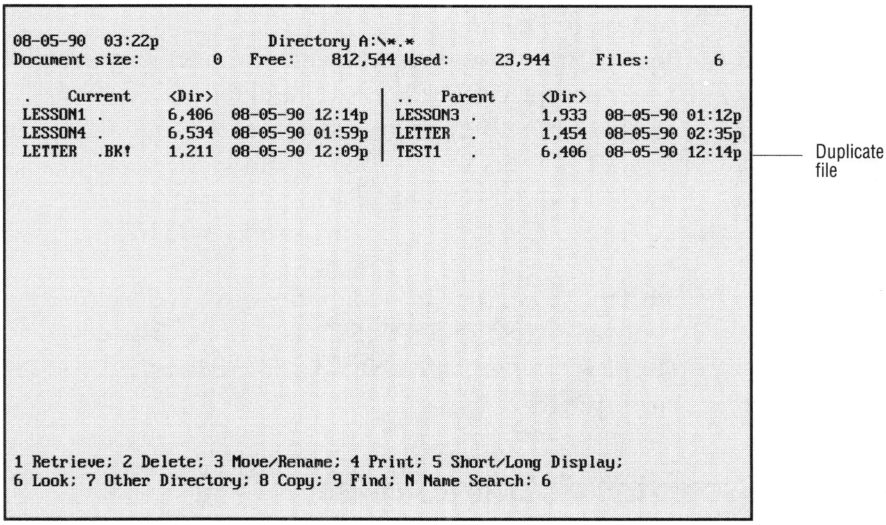

Figure 6-2:
A Duplicate Copy

thing like Figure 6-2.

Marking Files

A quick way to move more than one file is to first mark the files you intend to move with an asterisk. Position the highlighted cursor on the file and press *. When you have marked all the files, you can then copy, move, or delete them using the appropriate option from the menu.

To unmark a file, mark it with an asterisk a second time. This procedure will remove the first asterisk.

Renaming a Document

In this exercise, you will use the Move/Rename option to rename a document.

First, locate your TEST1 file by using the Name Search feature. You can invoke this feature by first using the List Files **[F5]** option, and then pressing **N** and typing in one or more letters of the file name you want to find.

To use the Name Search feature,

1. . . . .Press **N**
   Then to locate your TEST1 file,
2. . . . .Press **T**
   The cursor bar will move to the first file that starts with the letter T. If this file is not TEST1, type **E**, then **S**, then **T**, then **1**, if necessary, until the cursor bar moves onto TEST1.
   To stop the name search routine,
3. . . . .Press **[Enter]** or any of the cursor movement arrows.
   Note that the TEST1 file is still highlighted.
   To change the file's name using Move/Rename,
4. . . . .Press **3**
   The following prompt will appear on the status line:
   New name: A:TEST1

   With the cursor positioned on the drive A designation,
5. . . . .Type **A:\WP51\NEWTEST1** and press **[Enter]**
   TEST1 is now renamed NEWTEST1. To leave the List Files screen,
6. . . . .Press **[Exit]**

Creating Subdirectories

As you create and save files, you may discover that some of your files can be grouped together under common headings. You might have files which contain memos, or letters, or recipes, or just plain miscellaneous information. By creating these categories for listing files, you will be able to locate files much faster than if you listed them only by their major topic.

In this next exercise, where the default drive is A, you will create a subdirectory and copy a file into this subdirectory.

To create a new subdirectory, use the List Files command **[F5]** and then press option **7** for the Other Directory option.

1. . . . .Press **[F5]**
   If the prompt says **A:*.***, press **[Enter]**
   If the prompt says **C:\WP51*.***, type **A:** and press **[Enter]**
2. . . . .Press **7**
   You should see the following prompt on the status line:
   New directory = A:

   Move the cursor to the right of the \ and
3. . . . .Type **TEMP** and press **[Enter]**

The following prompt will appear on the status line:

Create A:\TEMP? No (**Y**es)

4.....Press **Y**

You have now created the TEMP subdirectory, which is one level under

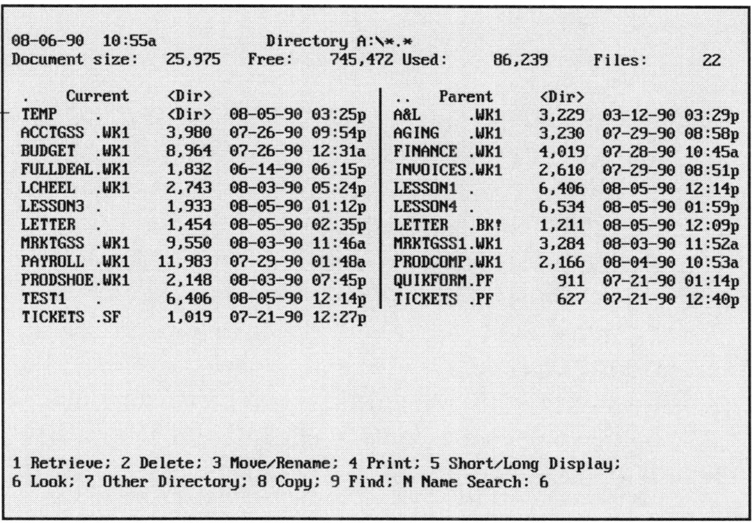


```
08-06-90  10:55a              Directory A:\*.*
Document size:    25,975   Free:     745,472 Used:       86,239      Files:        22

 .      Current    <Dir>                       |  ..      Parent     <Dir>
 TEMP      .       <Dir>   08-05-90 03:25p     |  A&L       .WK1     3,229  03-12-90 03:29p
 ACCTGSS  .WK1     3,980   07-26-90 09:54p     |  AGING     .WK1     3,230  07-29-90 08:58p
 BUDGET   .WK1     8,964   07-26-90 12:31a     |  FINANCE  .WK1     4,019  07-28-90 10:45a
 FULLDEAL.WK1      1,832   06-14-90 06:15p     |  INVOICES.WK1      2,610  07-29-90 08:51p
 LCHEEL   .WK1     2,743   08-03-90 05:24p     |  LESSON1  .         6,406  08-05-90 12:14p
 LESSON3  .        1,933   08-05-90 01:12p     |  LESSON4  .         6,534  08-05-90 01:59p
 LETTER   .        1,454   08-05-90 02:35p     |  LETTER   .BK!      1,211  08-05-90 12:09p
 MRKTGSS  .WK1     9,550   08-03-90 11:46a     |  MRKTGSS1.WK1      3,284  08-03-90 11:52a
 PAYROLL  .WK1    11,983   07-29-90 01:48a     |  PRODCOMP.WK1      2,166  08-04-90 10:53a
 PRODSHOE.WK1      2,148   08-03-90 07:45p     |  QUIKFORM.PF         911  07-21-90 01:14p
 TEST1    .        6,406   08-05-90 12:14p     |  TICKETS  .PF        627  07-21-90 12:40p
 TICKETS  .SF      1,019   07-21-90 12:27p

1 Retrieve; 2 Delete; 3 Move/Rename; 4 Print; 5 Short/Long Display;
6 Look; 7 Other Directory; 8 Copy; 9 Find; N Name Search: 6
```

Figure 6-3: *New Directory Listed*

the main directory. When you request List Files, you will see the subdirectory listed as TEMP <DIR> as shown in Figure 6-3.

Copying Files

At this point the newly-created TEMP subdirectory is empty. Using the copy option **8**, you can place a copy of NEWTEST1 in a directory—in this case, in the TEMP subdirectory.

Position the highlight over the NEWTEST1 file.

1.....Press **8**

The following prompt will appear on the status line:

Copy this file to:

2.....Type **A:\TEMP** and press **[Enter]** to copy the NEWTEST1 file into the TEMP subdirectory.

To check the TEMP subdirectory to see if it contains the copied file, position the highlight on the TEMP and

3.....Press **6** to choose the Look option.

When the following prompt appears on the status line:

Dir A:\TEMP*.*

4.....Press **[Enter]**

The file listing for subdirectory TEMP will appear on the screen. The highlight will go to the word Parent in the files listing.

With the cursor on Parent <DIR>, press the Look option and then the [Enter] key to return to the main directory.

If you position the highlight on a file in the file listing rather than on a subdirectory, and press **6** for the Look option, the following message will appear on the status line:

Look: 1 Next Doc; **2 P**rev Doc: **0**

The first page of the highlighted file will be displayed on the screen. Whenever you press **1** or **[PgDn]**, you will move to the next file in the alphabetical listing of the files. Conversely, whenever you press **2** or **[PgUp]**, you will move to the file immediately ahead of the current document. Pressing **1** or **2** will cause the first page of each document to be displayed, so that you will be able to determine if the file is the one you want.

When you use the Look option, you may use only the up and down arrows for cursor movement to examine pages other than the first page of the file. The status line will remain as shown above until you exit this feature.

To exit the Look option, press the **[Exit]** or the zero **(0)** key.

Return to the main directory.

Deleting Files

You can delete files by using the Delete option **2** of the List Files **[F5]** command. In this exercise, you will erase the subdirectory TEMP, and the files TEST1 and NEWTEST1.

To delete the TEMP <DIR>, position the highlighted cursor on the TEMP and

1. . . . .Press **2**

   When the following prompt appears on the status line:

   Delete A:\TEMP? No (**Y**es)

2. . . . .Press **Y**

   Because the subdirectory contains files the following message will appear briefly on the status line:

   ERROR: Directory not empty

The List Files menu will reappear at the bottom of the screen. Before you can delete a subdirectory, you must first erase the files it contains. Therefore, you will have to change to the TEMP subdirectory to erase the NEWTEST1 file.

With the highlighted cursor positioned on the TEMP <DIR>

1. . . . .Press **7** **[Enter]** **[Enter]** to move to the TEMP subdirectory.

To erase the NEWTEST1 file, position the highlighted cursor on the NEWTEST1 file and

2. . . . .Press **2**

The following prompt appears on the status line:

Delete A:\TEMP\NEWTEST1? No (**Y**es)

3. . . . .Press **Y**

Now that you have erased subdirectory TEMP's files, you need to return to the former screen to erase the TEMP <DIR>.

Position the cursor bar on Parent <DIR> and

4. . . . .Press **7** **[Enter]** **[Enter]** to return to the Parent <DIR> on Drive A.

To position the cursor bar on TEMP <DIR>

5. . . . .Press **2**

When the following prompt appears on the status line:

Delete A:\TEMP? No (**Y**es)

6. . . . .Press **Y**

Position the cursor bar on NEWTEST1 and repeat the last two steps. To leave the List Files screen,

7. . . . .Press **[F7]**

Listing Specific Files

The List Files menu can fill up with files rather quickly. However, WordPerfect provides a way for you to display only those files that you want to work with at any given time.

In the following exercise, you will display only those files that begin with the letter "P."

1. . . . .Press **[F5]**

When you see the following prompt on the status line:

Dir A:*.* (Type = to change default Dir)

To display only those files which begin with the letter "P,"

2. . . . .Type **A:P*.*** and press **[Enter]**

(The asterisk (*), called a wildcard, represents all characters. By using it after the "P," you are instructing the program to find all file names that begin with "P" but allowing it to include any other characters following the "P" as shown in Figure 6-4.)

To return to the edit screen,

3. . . . .Press **[Space]**

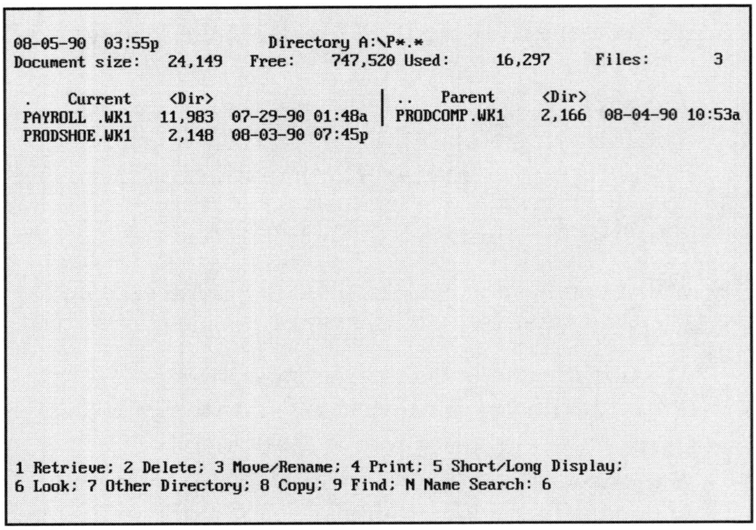

Figure 6-4:
Listing Files Starting with "P"

Searching Files in a Directory

So far, you have used the List Files key to display files in a directory or to display only certain files based on their file names. To help you find the right file, WordPerfect also allows you to search the contents of a file. If you need to retrieve a specific document but cannot tell which document you want simply by looking at the files in List Files, you can search for a key word contained in the file.

In the following exercise, you will attempt to find a file that refers to the Aromax Company.

1. . . . .Press **[F5]** and press **[Enter]**
   If the prompt says **Dir A:*.***, press **[Enter]**
   If the prompt says **Dir C:\WP51*.***, type **A:** and press **[Enter]**
   To select the option within Find that will search the entire document,
2. . . . .Press **9, 4**
   When the following prompt appears on the status line:

   Word pattern:

3. . . . .Type **aromax** and press **[Enter]**

When the computer has finished searching all of the files, it will list on the screen only those files that contain the word "Aromax."

4. . . . .Press **[F7]** to leave List Files.

NOTE: WordPerfect searches only the first ten pages of a file when the Entire Document option is requested. If the word sought, called a "search string," is not found in the first ten pages, but is contained in subsequent pages, WordPerfect will not list the file as containing that string of characters.

Finding Files in Another Subdirectory

To manage your files properly, you will probably need several subdirectories. You may, for example, decide to create a subdirectory for each important project or client. WordPerfect allows you to move easily from one subdirectory to another.

1.....To move to an existing subdirectory, you would press **[F5]**. The List Files would show you existing directories.
2.....If the prompt said **Dir A:*.***, you would press **[Enter]**
3.....If the prompt said **Dir C:\WP51*.***, you would type **A:** and press **[Enter]**
The List Files screen would appear showing all files and subdirectories on the data disk.
Earlier you used the Other Directory option to create a new subdirectory. You can also use it to change to a different subdirectory.
4.....You would press **7** to go to another directory.
The following prompt would appear on the status line:

New directory = A:\MEMO

5.....If you pressed **[Enter]** at this point, the following prompt would appear on the status line:

Dir A:\MEMO*.*

6.....If you wanted to see the files in that subdirectory, you would press **[Enter]**, and the files in the subdirectory would be displayed.

At this point you could select a file to retrieve to current memory or press the space bar to return to the current document.

General Exercises

1. Create a subdirectory on your student data disk labeled PRACTICE.
2. Copy all of your practice files to the PRACTICE subdirectory. The files should all begin with the letters PRAC.
3. Using the Word Search function, locate the files that contain the name "Alice Heldt." How many files are there?
4. If you intend to go on to another set of exercises, clear the screen. If not, exit WordPerfect.

Course-Specific Exercises

Group A Accounting

1. Load WordPerfect if necessary. List all files beginning with the letter A.
2. Find out how many files contain the word
   A. manager

B. assets

C. decision

3. Create a subdirectory labeled LEDGER.
4. Copy all ACCTG.* files to the LEDGER subdirectory.
5. Erase all files in the LEDGER subdirectory.
6. Delete the LEDGER subdirectory.
7. If you intend to go on to another set of exercises, clear the screen. If not, exit WordPerfect.

Group B Marketing

1. Load WordPerfect if necessary. List all files beginning with the letter M.
2. Find out how many files contain the word

   A. price

   B. promotion

   C. management

3. Create a subdirectory labeled SALES.
4. Copy all MARKTNG.* files to the SALES subdirectory.
5. Erase all files in the SALES subdirectory.
6. Delete the SALES subdirectory.
7. If you intend to go on to another set of exercises, clear the screen. If not, exit WordPerfect.

Group C Finance

1. Load WordPerfect if necessary. List all files beginning with the letter F.
2. Find out how many files contain the word

   A. decision maker

   B. manager

   C. financial

3. Create a subdirectory labeled BONDS.
4. Copy all FINANCE.* files to the BONDS subdirectory.
5. Erase all files in the BONDS subdirectory.
6. Delete the BONDS subdirectory.
7. If you intend to go on to another set of exercises, clear the screen. If not, exit WordPerfect.

Group D Production

1. Load WordPerfect if necessary. List all files beginning with the letter P. Find out how many files contain the word

   A. product

   B. JIT

C. Just-In-Time

3. Create a subdirectory labeled MANUFACT.
4. Copy all PRODUCT.* files to the MANUFACT subdirectory.
5. Erase all files in the MANUFACT subdirectory.
6. Delete the MANUFACT subdirectory.
7. Exit WordPerfect.

7

Macros

The objectives of this lesson are to

- Create a macro
- Use a macro

Creating Macros

A macro is a sequence of keystrokes saved in a special file so that you can use it again whenever you wish, just by typing the few keystrokes assigned to it. Whenever you find yourself repeatedly typing a sequence of commands or a word, phrase or paragraph, you should consider creating a macro.

In this exercise, you will create a macro to type the following company letterhead and the current date:

SOLAR DISTILLATION INDUSTRIES
1340 EAST BROADWAY
TUCSON, ARIZONA 85692

1.....Press **[Ctrl]+[F10]**
When the following prompt appears on the status line:
Define macro:

2.....Press **[Alt]+L** to define the sequence of keys which when used later will retrieve and execute the macro.
The following message will appear on the status line:
Description:

3.....Type **LETTERHEAD AND CURRENT DATE** and press **[Enter]**
The following blinking prompt will appear on the status line:
Macro Def

This message means that any keys you press from now until you turn off the Macro Definition feature will be recorded as part of the macro, so be careful!

4. . . . .Type the following heading:

SOLAR DISTILLATION INDUSTRIES
1340 EAST BROADWAY
TUCSON, ARIZONA 85692

Position the cursor on the "S" of "Solar" in the first line. To activate the Blocking feature in order to center the heading,

5. . . . .Press **[Alt]+[F4]** or **[F12]**

Move the cursor one space to the right of the last digit in the zip code.

6. . . . .Press **[Shift]+[F6]**

When the following prompt appears on the status line:

[Just:Center]? No (**Y**es)

7. . . . .Type **Y** to center the entire heading.

To position the cursor for selecting the current date code,

8. . . . .Press **[Enter] [Enter] [Enter]**

To select the command to automatically insert the current date,

9. . . . .Press **[Shift]+[F5]**, **2**

To stop the Macro Definition command,

10. . . .Press **[Ctrl]+[F10]** and the macro is automatically saved.

Clear the screen.

Using a Macro

Before you use a macro that you have created, you need to position the cursor at the point in the document where you want the results of the macro to appear.

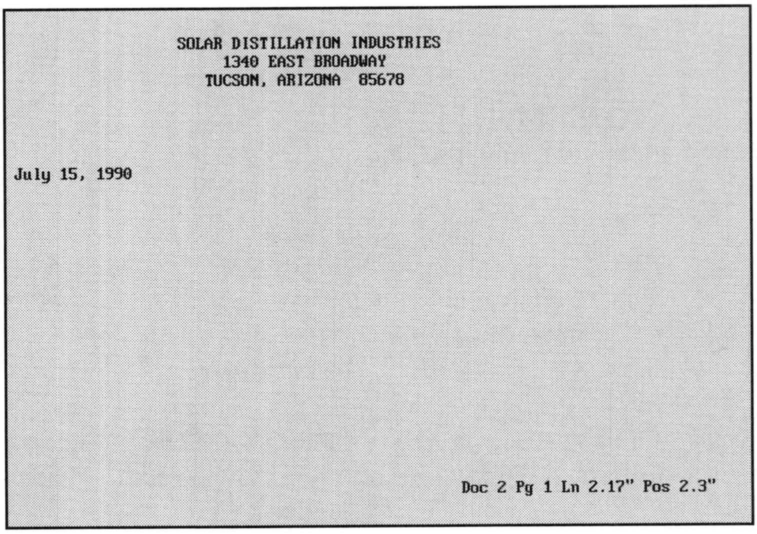

Figure 7-1: *Result of Invoking the Macro*

To use the macro you created in the previous exercise to print the letterhead and current date, position the cursor at the top left of the screen and

1. . . . .Press **[Alt]+L**

The letterhead with the current date similar to that shown in Figure 7-1 will appear on the screen.

Clear the screen.

General Exercises

1. Load WordPerfect if necessary. Create a macro using the definition [Alt]+C which when invoked creates the following closing for a letter:

   Sincerely yours,

   (your name)

   Production Associate

   cc: J. Towers

   M. Peden

   S. Salehi

2. Create a macro using the definition [Alt]+V to choose option 6 (View Document) of the Print menu.
3. Create a macro using the definition [Alt]+M to create a memo with a bold capitalized heading **MEMO** and the current date.
4. Create a macro using the definition [Alt]+S to save any file on screen as A:LASTCOPY to the student data disk and prepare to exit WordPerfect.
5. Create a macro using the definition [Alt]+R to retrieve the LASTCOPY file on the student data disk.
6. If you intend to go on to another set of exercises, clear the screen. If not, exit WordPerfect.

Course-Specific Exercises

Group A Accounting

1. Load WordPerfect if necessary. Create a macro to reproduce the following memo. Define it as [Alt]+X.

2. Clear the screen.

MEMORANDUM

To:
From:
Date:
Subject:

3. Use the macro to create a short memo of any subject you wish.
4. Save the memo as A:MEMO2.
5. If you intend to go on to another set of exercises, clear the screen. If not, exit WordPerfect.

Group B Marketing

1. Load WordPerfect if necessary. Create a macro to reproduce the following communication summary for a billing advertisement insert. Define it as [Alt]+B.

Bill Communication Summary

Dates Mailing: ____________________ Insert/Message: __________

Title: ____________________ Number of Pieces: _______

Audience: ____________________ Weight of Pieces: ________

Sponsor: ____________________

Comments____

____

____

2. Clear the screen.
3. Use the macro to create a summary filled in as you wish.
4. Save the form as A:BILL.
5. If you intend to go on to another set of exercises, clear the screen. If not, exit WordPerfect.

Group C Finance

1. Load WordPerfect if necessary. Create a macro to reproduce the following table of ratios. Define it as [Alt]+F.
2. Clear the screen.
3. Use the macro and fill in some values in the Value column.
4. Save the filled in form as A:RATIOS.
5. If you intend to go on to another set of exercises, clear the screen. If not, exit WordPerfect.

S & M Publishers
Current Financial Ratios

	RATIO	VALUE
1.	Accounts Receivable Turnover	
	Annual Credit Sales / Accounts Receivable	
2.	Inventory Turnover	
	Sales / Inventory of Finished Goods	
3.	Net Profit Margin	
	Profits after Taxes / Sales	
4.	Quick Ratio	
	Current Assets – Inventory / Current Liabilities	
5.	Return on Stockholders' Equity	
	Profits After Taxes / Total Stockholders' Equity	

Group D Production

1. Load WordPerfect if necessary. Create a macro to reproduce the following communication for computer programming requests. Define it as [Alt]+Y.

Title:

Sponsor:

Beginning Cycle: Date:

Ending Cycle: Date:

Recipients:
- **ZIP codes -**
- **Grids -**
- **Codes -**

Type:

2. Clear the screen.
3. Use the macro and fill in the form with any information you wish.
4. Save the form as A:REQUEST.
5. Clear the screen and exit WordPerfect.

8

Graphics

The objectives of this lesson are to

- Use graphics in a document
- Create a graphics box
- Place a graphics box inside another graphics box
- Edit the graphics figure and text
- Edit the graphics box through the use of options
- Create and position horizontal and vertical lines

Using Graphics

Graphics are a form of art which can be incorporated into the text material of a document. The use of graphics enhances the appearance of the document. Until quite recently, this mixture of text and graphics was available only through typesetting. Now, however, WordPerfect allows you to enhance documents with visual aids, whether pictures or lines. The lines can be either horizontal or vertical.

You can position a graphics box in headers, footers, footnotes, and endnotes, as well as in the main body of the text. You can also place one or more graphics boxes on top of another.

NOTE: You should have a graphics card installed in your microcomputer to take full advantage of the capabilities of WordPerfect graphics. Your printer should also be capable of supporting the graphics feature.

Creating a Graphics Box

You must create a graphics box by using the command **[Alt] + [F9]** before you retrieve a file with a WordPerfect Graphics extension (.WPG). The clip art pictures included with the WordPerfect software all have .WPG extensions.

Creating a graphics box is a simple task. In this exercise you will use the picture of the butterfly, which is usually located in the WP51 directory, saved under the file name BUTTRFLY.WPG. Load WordPerfect and go to a cleared screen.

1.....Press **[Alt]+[F9]** to select the Graphics feature.
When the following menu appears on the status line:
1 Figure; **2 T**able Box; **3** Text **B**ox; **4 U**ser Box; **5 L**ine; **6 E**quation: **0**

2.....Press **1** or **F** to select the Figure option.
When the following menu appears on the status line:
Figure: 1 Create; **2 E**dit; **3 N**ew Number; **4 O**ption: **0**

3.....Press **1** or **C** to select the Create option.
4.....Press **1** to select the Filename option.
5.....Type **C:\WP51\BUTTRFLY.WPG** and press **[Enter]**
6.....Press **[F7]** to exit from the Graphics feature and return to the document.

You will see a representation of where the graphic will appear on the screen as the top of a box labeled FIG 1. The rest of the box will appear if you press [Enter] repeatedly to insert lines down the screen. Note that the actual graphic is not shown on the screen, but rather only its box is given. Note also that the computer has numbered the graphics box. You can refer to that box number to make any modification of the parameters.

Editing Graphics

It is important to remember that there are two sets of menu options that help you to modify graphics: the box within which the graphics is placed, and the graphic, or the text, or the equation itself. To change the box, choose the Options menu. The Options menu allows you to change the border of the box, the margins both inside and outside the box, as well as the caption placement and numbering system. In addition, you can control the degree of shading in the figure from the Options menu.

You can also use the Edit option in the Graphic feature to change the default values of the graphics box. The Edit option controls characteristics such as the size of the box, its placement on the page, and the positioning within the box. Through the Edit option in the default values, you can invert, scale and rotate a graphics figure as well as create a mirror image. If you are using a text box, you can determine the text, the font and positioning of the text.

Using the Graphics Box Option

In this exercise, you will change the border style from the single line as shown in Figure 8-1 to double lines. Using Reveal Codes, position the cursor on [Fig Box:1; BUTTRFLY.WPG;] in the BUTTRFLY file and,

1.....Press **[Alt]+[F9]**

From the menu that appears,

2.....Press **1** to select Figure.

3.....Press **4** for Options.

To change the border style from the menu shown in Figure 8-1,

```
Options: Figure

     1 - Border Style
              Left                        Single
              Right                       Single
              Top                         Single
              Bottom                      Single
     2 - Outside Border Space
              Left                        0.167"
              Right                       0.167"
              Top                         0.167"
              Bottom                      0.167"
     3 - Inside Border Space
              Left                        0"
              Right                       0"
              Top                         0"
              Bottom                      0"
     4 - First Level Numbering Method     Numbers
     5 - Second Level Numbering Method    Off
     6 - Caption Number Style             [BOLD]Figure 1[bold]
     7 - Position of Caption              Below box, Outside borders
     8 - Minimum Offset from Paragraph    0"
     9 - Gray Shading (% of black)        0%

Selection: 0
```

Figure 8-1: *Graphics Box Options*

4.....Press **1**

for Border Style.

The cursor will move to the style for the left border, which in Figure 8-1 is single. To change to a double line for the border on all sides:

5.....Press **3** four times.

You can make changes to any of the other options shown on the menu in Figure 8-1 at this time. When you have made all of the changes you intend to make,

6.....Press **[F7]** to return to the document.

You can verify changes to the graphics box border by invoking the View option of the Print command. Whenever you use the Options feature for a graphics box, the code [Fig Opt] will precede the code indicating the use of a graphics box. If more than one [Fig Opt] code is present, only the one to the immediate left of the graphics box applies.

To view the changes you made in the graphics box border,

1.....Press **[Shift] + [F7]**

2. . . . .Press **6** or **V** for View.
The butterfly graphic with double lines around it now appears on the screen.
3. . . . .Press **[F7]** to leave View Document.

Using the Edit Option

After creating the graphics box, and viewing the graphic by pressing **[Shift]+[F7], 6**, you can change the box. If you do not like a certain aspect of the box, such as the left to right placement, you can change this feature. If the box is too small, you can enlarge it. If the box is too large, you can reduce it. If you want the graphic to point in a different direction, you can change its orientation. If you want a mirror image, you can reverse the box.

In this exercise, you will center the graphics box between the left and right margins. You will also make the graphics box five inches wide.

Using Reveal Codes, position the highlighted cursor on the Graphics box code [Fig Box: 1; BUTTRFLY.WPG;] and

1. . . . .Press **[Alt]+[F9]** to use the Graphics feature.
2. . . . .Press **1** to select Figure.
3. . . . .Press **2** to select the Edit option.
4. . . . .Press **[Enter]** to confirm that you want to use graphics box Figure 1.
If you have accidentally chosen the wrong style box, you will see the message ***Not Found***.
5. . . . .Press **6**
When the following menu for positioning the figure appears:
Horizontal Position: 1 Left; **2 R**ight; **3 C**enter; **4 F**ull: **0**

6. . . . .Press **3** to center the figure on the page.
The results of your selection will become immediately apparent when you are in option **6**.
7. . . . .Press **7** to change size.
When the following menu appears:
1 Set **W**idth/Auto Height; **2** Set **H**eight/Auto Width; **3** Set **B**oth; **4 A**uto Both: **0**

8. . . . .Press **1** to set the width and let the computer automatically set the height.
9. . . . .Type **5.** and press **[Enter]** to set a width of 5. The computer will automatically establish a proportional height of 3.63 inches.
10. . . .Press **[Enter]** to return to the document.
11. . . .Press **[Alt] + [F3]** to turn off Reveal Codes.

You have now changed the graphic's parameters. You can view these changes by invoking the View option of the Print command.

Clear the screen. Do not save the file.

Placing Graphics in Graphics

Now that you have learned the basics of creating and editing a graphics box, you should find placing one graphics box inside another a fairly simple task.

Using the available clip-art supplied by WordPerfect, in this exercise you will place the butterfly graphic inside the graphics file labeled BORDER-3, center the graphic between the left and right margins, and remove all borders.

1.....Press **[Alt]+[F9], 1, 1, 1**
To retrieve the border graphics file,
2.....Type **C:\WP51\BORDER-8.WPG** and press **[Enter]**
To center the graphic between the margins,
3.....Press **6, 3**
To create a box 4.5 inches wide,
4.....Press **7, 1**
5.....Type **4.5** and press **[Enter]**
6.....Press **8**
The next step is important because it allows you to place the second graphics box over the first one. When you press 8, the prompt gives you the option

Wrap Text Around Box Yes (**No**).

It is absolutely essential that you respond No. Therefore,
7.....Press **N**
To see what the border graphics file looks like,
8.....Press **9**
To return to the document,
9.....Press **[F7]** twice.

When you select a given option for a graphics figure, those parameters remain in effect until you change them. In this part of the exercise, you will eliminate the graphics box borders, set the inside and outside margin spaces to 0 (zero), and set the shading to 0 (zero) percent.

Use Reveal Codes to position the cursor on the graphics box code for the BORDER-8 file.

1.....Press **[Alt]+[F9], 1, 4, 1**
To change the border style to None,
2.....Press **1** four times.
To set the four outside border spaces to 0 (zero),
3.....Press **2** to go to outside border space.
4.....Press the **0, [Enter]** combination four times.
To set the Gray Shading percentage to 0 (zero),
5.....Press **9, 0, [Enter]**
To return to the document,
6.....Press **[Enter]** twice.

Use the View option of the Print command to examine the graphics.

To add the second graphics box to the inside of the first one, position the cursor immediately to the right of the code for the graphics box and

1.....Press **[Alt]+[F9], 1, 1, 1**
To retrieve the butterfly graphic file,
2.....Type **C:\WP51\BUTTRFLY.WPG** and press **[Enter]**
To go to the Edit option to place the butterfly graphic over the first graphics box,
3.....Press **6, 3** to center the box between the left and right margins.
To make this graphic slightly smaller than the first graphic,
4.....Press **7, 1**
5.....Type **4.** and press **[Enter]**
This will make the second box a half-inch narrower than the first box.
As before, to set the option Wrap Text Around Box to No,
6.....Press **8, N**

Return to the document and examine the results using the View option of the Print command. When you do so, you will find that the butterfly is positioned too high in the graphics box for symmetry and therefore should be lowered. The way to reposition the second graphics box is by using the Advance command.

Using the Advance Command

You can use the Advance command **[Shift] + [F8], 4** to position text to an exact spot on the page, as well as to position a graphics box. To reposition the butterfly graphics box, use Reveal Codes to place the cursor on the code for the butterfly. You will execute the Advance command before you position the second graphics box on the first box.

It appears that you should lower the butterfly box about a quarter of an inch. With the cursor on the code for the butterfly,

1.....Press **[Shift]+[F8], 4** to select the Format which contains the Advance command.
2.....Press **1, 2** to specify the direction Down.
After you have chosen the direction,
3.....Type **.25** and press **[Enter]** to specify the exact distance you want to move the figure before the computer executes the next operation.
To return to the document,
4.....Press **[Enter]** twice.

Check the positioning of the two graphics boxes using the View option of the Print command. Readjust the butterfly box if necessary.

Print the document. Save the document as A:GRAFGRAF and clear the screen.

Placing Text in Graphics

Besides placing one graphics box within another graphics box, you can also place text within a graphics box to personalize your graphics.

In this exercise, you will use the trophy graphics file and place the following message on the trophy's plate:

Dedicated to

WP CLASS OF 94

1.....Press **[Alt] + [F9]**, **1, 1, 1**
2.....Type **C:WP51\TROPHY.WPG**
3.....Press **6, 3** to center the graphics box.
4.....Press **8, N** to not wrap text (That is, to place the text inside the box).
5.....Press **7, 1**
6.....Type **6.5** and press **[Enter]**
To view the graphics box and to make the desired changes,
7.....Press **9**

Because the plate on the trophy's base is not large enough to hold the above message, you need to enlarge the graphic. You can use the scale feature to change the width and height of the graphic.

8.....Press **2**
When the prompt for Scale X appears,
9.....Type **140** and press **[Enter]**
When the prompt requesting a change in the Y-axis appears,
10....Type **120** and press **[Enter]**
To return to the document,
11....Press **[Enter]** twice.

Now that you have adjusted the graphic's size, you can create a text box to contain the above message.

1.....Press **[Alt]+[F9], 3, 1, 9**
The following prompt appears:
Box: Press **E**xit when done, **G**raphics to rotate the text

2.....Press **[Shift] + [F6]** and enter the text as shown at the start of this exercise.
3.....Press **[F7]** to return to the Edit menu for the Text box.
4.....Press **6, 3** to center the box between the left and right margins.
The plate's graphics box will require a size of 3 inches by 1 inch.
5.....Press **7, 3** to obtain the Set Both option from the menu for setting height and width.
To set the width at 3 inches,
6.....Type **3.** and press **[Enter]**
To set the height at 1 inch,
7.....Type **1.** and press **[Enter]**

To set the option Wrap Text Around Box to No,

8.....Press **8, N**

To return to the document,

9.....Press **[Enter]**

When you use the View option of the Print command to examine the document, you will notice two problems: the text is too high, and the borders and the background shading of the text box are visible.

To set the borders, outside margin spaces, and gray shading to 0, use the procedure outlined in the section Placing Graphics in Graphics. To go to the Text Box options,

1.....Press **[Alt]+[F9], 3, 4**

Make the appropriate changes in the Options menu. Return to the document and use the View option of the Print command to view the results of these changes. You will find that only the placement problem remains. To correctly position the text, use the Advance command procedure and set the down distance to 4.0 inches.

Use the View option to examine the finished product. Make any necessary adjustments. Save the file as A:GRPH_TXT and clear the screen.

Creating Graphics Lines

WordPerfect's graphics feature allows you to create and edit, if necessary, both horizontal and vertical lines. These single lines have no relationship to the borders around the graphics boxes. You can place these lines at the position of the cursor, or you can position them through the menu.

In this exercise, you will place a horizontal line from left margin to right margin 1.5 inches below the text box position. Retrieve your A:GRPH_TXT file and, using Reveal Codes, position the cursor immediately to the right of the text box code [Txt Opt] to use the Advance command to position the cursor 1.5 inches down from the text box

1.....Press **[Shift]+[F8], 4, 1, 2**

2.....Type **1.5** and press **[Enter]**

3.....Press **[Enter]** twice to return to the document.

Use the following procedure to create a horizontal line:

1.....Press **[Alt]+[F9]** to go to the Graphics mode.

From the menu on the status line,

2.....Press **5** to select the Line option.

To create the horizontal line,

3.....Press **1**

The menu shown in Figure 8-2 will appear.

From this menu, selecting Full for option 1 ensures that the horizontal line will stretch from the left margin to the right margin. For option 2,

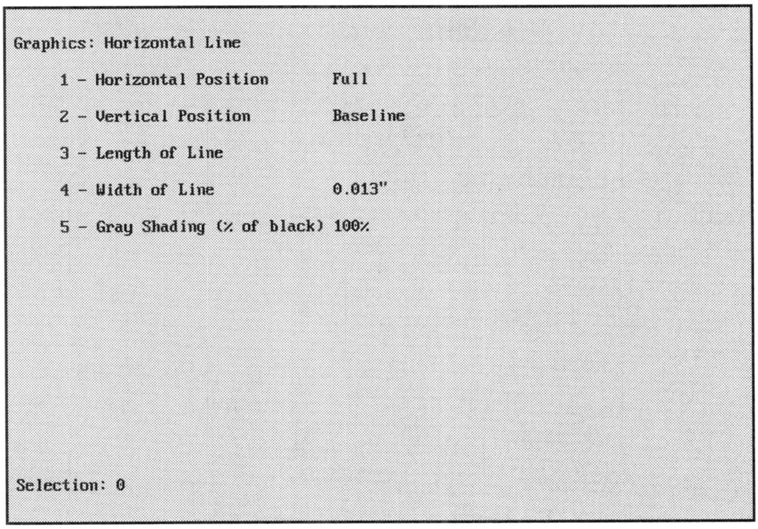

Figure 8-2:
A Graphics Line Menu

the selection of Baseline means that the horizontal line will be placed at the position of the cursor. You will use option 3 only if you select an option other than Full for 1. Option 4 allows you to vary the thickness of the horizontal line.

To show the effect of option 4,

4.....Press **4**

To change the thickness of the line,

5.....Type **.02** and press **[Enter]**

6.....Press **[Enter]** 2 twice to return to the document.

Use the View Document option to examine the document.

Do not save file. Clear the screen.

In the same manner, you can create vertical lines. The submenus that appear as you select the various options are informative. Do not forget to use the Help command **[F3]** if you need assistance.

General Exercises

In all of the following problems, make the finished product pleasing to the eye.

1. Load WordPerfect if necessary. Retrieve the graphics file ARROW-22.WPG.
   - A. Change the width of the graphics box to 5 inches and add the text "UP" within the arrow. Remove all borders. Print the completed graphic.
   - B. Invert or rotate the arrow 180 degrees and change the "UP" to "DOWN." Print the completed graphic.
   - C. Rotate the arrow 90 degrees and change the text to "ONE WAY." Print the completed graphic.
2. Clear the screen and retrieve the graphics file PRESNT-1.WPG.

A. Place the GLOBE2-M.WPG file inside the borders of the blackboard in the PRESNT-1.WPG file. Print the completed graphic.
B. Replace the GLOBE2-M.WPG file with the FLOPPY-2.WPG file. Keep the FLOPPY-2 file within the borders of the blackboard. Print the completed graphic.

3. Clear the screen and retrieve the graphics file PRESNT-1.WPG.
   A. Position the CNTRCT-2.WPG file within the borders of the blackboard. Remove the borders on the CNTRCT-2.WPG file. Print the completed graphics.
   B. With the CNTRCT-2.WPG file properly positioned, add a text box that says "CONTRACTS." Keep the text above the bottom edge of the blackboard but below the graphics picture of the document. In addition to using the Advance command, changing the left or right margins may help you position the text. Print the completed graphic.
4. Clear the screen and create a .04 inch border all around the page's margins.
5. Clear the screen and create a .05 inch left-hand border from the top to bottom margins.
6. Clear the screen and center the heading "Table of Contents." Center a 4-inch-long horizontal line approximately .25 inches below the heading.
7. If you intend to go on to another set of exercises, clear the screen. If not, exit WordPerfect.

Course-Specific Exercises

Group A Accounting

1. Load WordPerfect if necessary. Retrieve and center the graphics file SCALE.WPG and place the words "ASSETS" and "LIABILITIES" on the

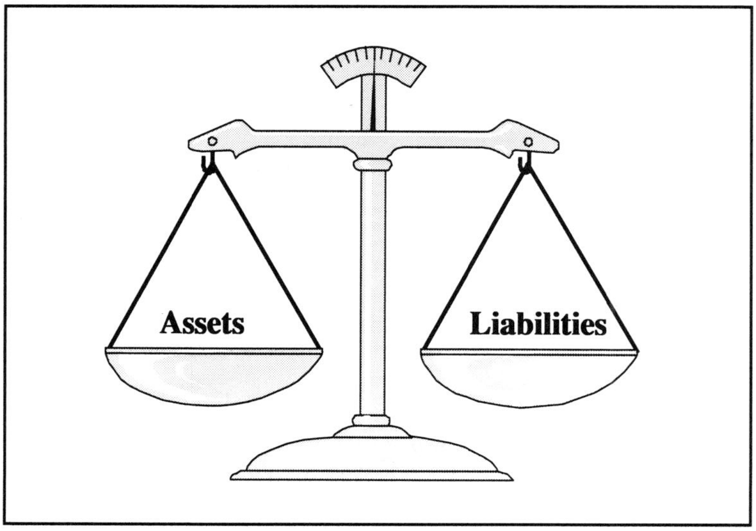

SCALE.WPG

platforms of the scale. Make the SCALE.WPG file 4 inches wide. Print the completed graphic.
2. Reposition the graphic created above against the right-hand margin. Print the completed graphic.
3. Reposition the graphic created in Problem 1 against the left-hand margin. Print the completed graphic.
4. Center the SCALE.WPG file and change option 6 of the Figure Definition menu to Full. Print the completed graphic.
5. If you intend to go on to another set of exercises, clear the screen. If not, exit WordPerfect.

Group B Marketing

1. Load WordPerfect if necessary. Retrieve and center the graphics file MAILBAG.WPG and place the text "ORDERS POURING IN!" below the picture but within the graphics box. Set the MAILBAG.WPG file to a 4 inch width. Print the completed graphic.

MAILBAG.WPG

2. Reposition the graphic created above against the right-hand margin. Print the completed graphic.
3. Reposition the graphic created in Problem 1 against the left-hand margin. Print the completed graphic.
4. Center the MAILBAG.WPG file and change option 6 of the Figure Definition menu to Full. Print the completed graphic.
5. If you intend to go on to another set of exercises, clear the screen. If not, exit WordPerfect.

Group C Finance

1. Load WordPerfect if necessary. Retrieve and center the graphics file NEWS.WPG and place the text "Good News on Wall Street" below the paper but within the graphic. Set the NEWS.WPG file to a 4-inch width. (You might have to move the newspaper up within the graphics box.) Print the completed graphic.

NEWS.WPG

2. Reposition the graphic created above against the right-hand margin. Print the completed graphic.
3. Reposition the graphic created in Problem 1 against the left-hand margin. Print the completed graphic.
4. Center the NEWS.WPG file and change option 6 of the Figure Definition menu to Full. Print the completed graphic.
5. If you intend to go on to another set of exercises, clear the screen. If not, exit WordPerfect.

Group D Production

1. Load WordPerfect if necessary. Retrieve and center the graphics file DEVICE-2.WPG. Place the graphics file PC-1.WPG within the curtain of the DEVICE-2.WPG. Add the text "Announcing ZERO Defects" above the trumpet. Set the DEVICE-2.WPG file to a 4.5-inch width. Print the completed graphic.
2. Reposition the graphic created above against the right-hand margin. Print the completed graphic.

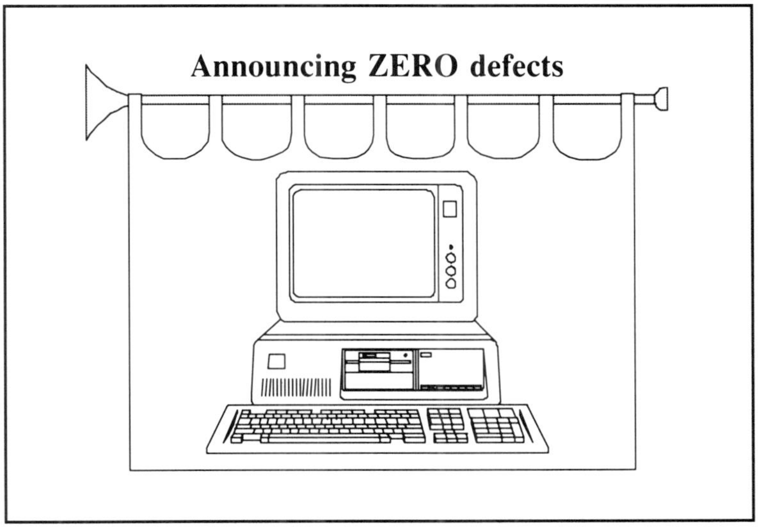

DEVICE-2.WPG

3. Reposition the graphic created in Problem 1 against the left-hand margin. Print the completed graphic.
4. Center the DEVICE-2.WPG file and change option 6 of the Figure Definition menu to Full. Print the completed graphic.
5. Exit WordPerfect.

9

Merging Documents

The objectives of this lesson are to

- Exit to DOS
- Set the time and date
- Merge primary and secondary files to create form letters that appear to be personalized for each recipient
- Create forms that can be filled in as needed

Merging

All organizations rely on files, especially the name and address file. Businesses use this file to send their customers advertisements, invoices and announcements, while professional organizations use it to announce meetings, seminars and to send membership renewal notices. If you work for such an organization or company, knowing how to merge the name and address file with other documents to create "personalized" notices will simplify your job. Typically, the name and address file is called a secondary file and the document it is merged with is known as the primary file, i.e. the form letter.

In this exercise, you will create primary and secondary files to produce form letters. You will first create the primary file for the merge. The variable data, that is, the date, the recipient's name and address, and the salutation will differ from letter to letter and will be represented by merge codes in the primary file. You will type the actual data—the names, addresses, etc.—and save them in a separate secondary file, from which you will retrieve them during the merge.

Exiting to DOS

The first step in this process requires you to exit to DOS. Each time you use the primary file document that you create, you will need to enter the current date. To make sure the computer will supply the correct date,

1.....Press **[Ctrl]+[F1]**
When the following prompt appears on the status line:
1 Go to DOS; **2** DOS **C**ommand: **0**

2.....Press **2** and WordPerfect will branch temporarily to the DOS system to execute a single command.
The following prompt will appear on the status line:
DOS Command:

3.....Type **DATE** and press **[Enter]** and WordPerfect will respond by showing the current date.
If the computer shows a current date that is not correct, enter the two digit code for the month, a dash, today's date, a dash, and two or four digits for the year.

4.....Press **[Enter]**
The following prompt will appear on the status line:
Press any key to continue

5.....Press **[Enter]** to return to the document.

If you intend to execute more than a single DOS function, you should choose option **1** to go to DOS, perform all of the actions required and then return to WordPerfect. The procedure for going to DOS is:

1.....Press **[Ctrl]+[F1]**
To select the DOS system,

2.....Press **1**

The WordPerfect document will disappear from the screen and new information about the computer will appear, as in Figure 9-1. The last two lines of this new information are the most important. These two lines are

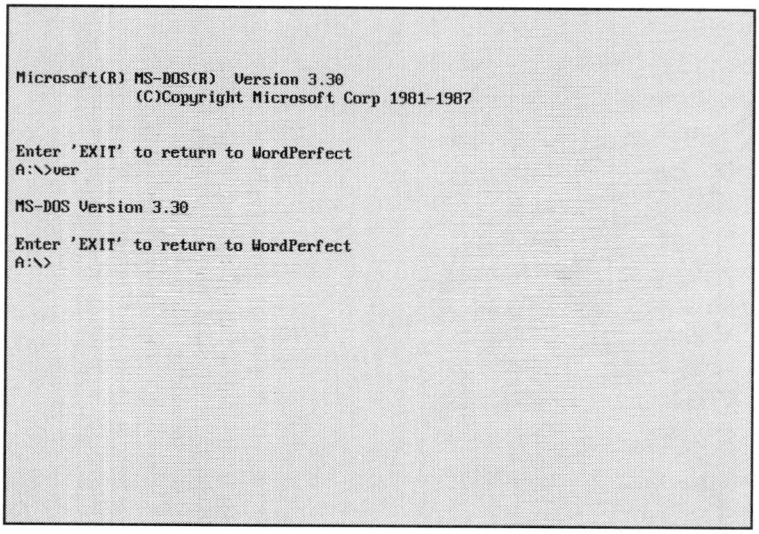

Figure 9-1:
In DOS Mode

Enter **EXIT** to return to WordPerfect
A: (or **C:\WP51** if you're using a hard disk drive)

At this point you can enter any DOS command you want. At the conclusion of that DOS command, the same two line message will appear. To return to WordPerfect and the exact location in the document where you initially exited to DOS,

3.....Type **EXIT** and press **[Enter]**

Creating Secondary Files

The secondary file you create will contain seven data fields that will be merged into the primary file (the form letter). Each field is a distinct piece of data such as a name, street, city, or zip code, and the actual data for each field will differ from letter to letter. Each group of seven data fields is called a record. Each record must contain the same number of fields, and the same relative position of each field within the record must contain the same type of information. The entire collection of records is called a file.

When you create a secondary file, you will establish a record format at the beginning of the file. In subsequent operations, you can refer to the fields by the name of the field or the field number in the record format. The field numbers begin with 1 and are numbered consecutively. The following example demonstrates the record format:

(field 1, buyer's full name)
(field 2, street address)
(field 3, city)
(field 4, state)
(field 5, zip code)
(field 6, title and last name)
(field 7, number of tickets)

To create the beginning format for the secondary file, clear the screen and position the cursor at the top.

1.....Press **[Shift]+[F9]**
When the following menu appears on the status line:
1 Field; **2 E**nd Record; **3 I**nput; **4 P**age; **5 N**ext Record; **6 M**ore: **0**

2.....Press **6**
Position the highlighted cursor on
{FIELD NAMES}name1~ . . . nameN~~

3.....Press **[Enter]**
When the following prompt appears on the status line:
Enter Field 1:

4. . . . .Type **buyer's full name** and press **[Enter]**
The prompt on the status line will change to the next field number. Repeat step 4 until all of the fields are entered as shown on the previous page and then

5. . . . .Press **[Enter]** a second time.
A double dashed line will appear across the screen to signal the end of the record format.

The completed record format will look like the example given in Figure 9-2. To make the record format more readable it has been reformatted as shown in Figure 9-3.

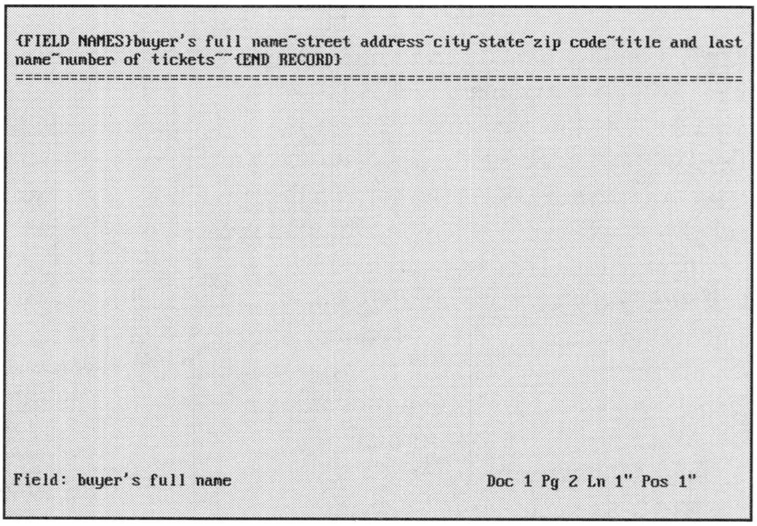

Figure 9-2: *Normal Record Format*

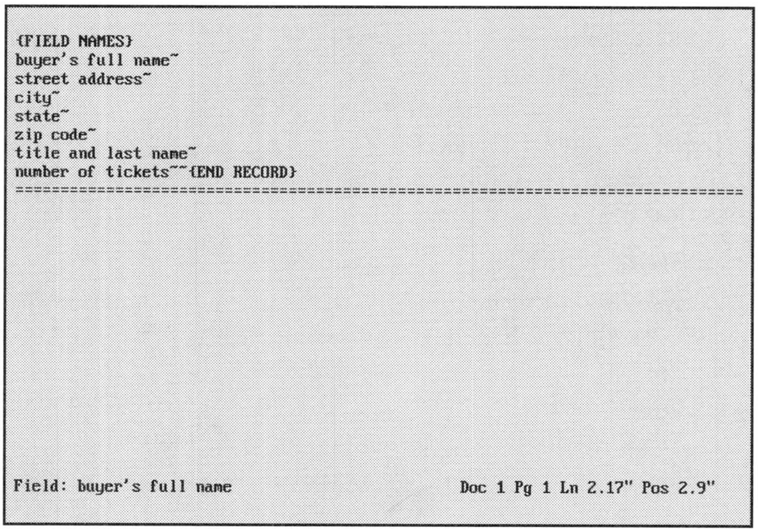

Figure 9-3: *Rearranged Record Format*

The file is now ready to accept data for the records to be placed in the secondary file. The prompt for field number 1 (buyer's full name) appears on the status line.

Entering Records in the Secondary File

The {END FIELD} code at the end of the field separates each field (name, city, etc.) in the secondary file. The {END RECORD} code marks each record (all the fields for a single form letter).

In the following exercise, you will enter the record

Mr. and Mrs. Sean Donovan
Building 78, Suite 21
1000 Skyline Blvd.
Seattle
WA
91232
Mr. and Mrs. Donovan
750

At the prompt of **Field 1:** on the status line,

1.....Type **Mr. and Mrs. Sean Donovan**

Do not press the [Enter] key at the end of the line except to create additional lines of text for the field. (See Figure 9-4.) Instead, you will use the End Field **[F9]** key.

2.....Press **[F9]**

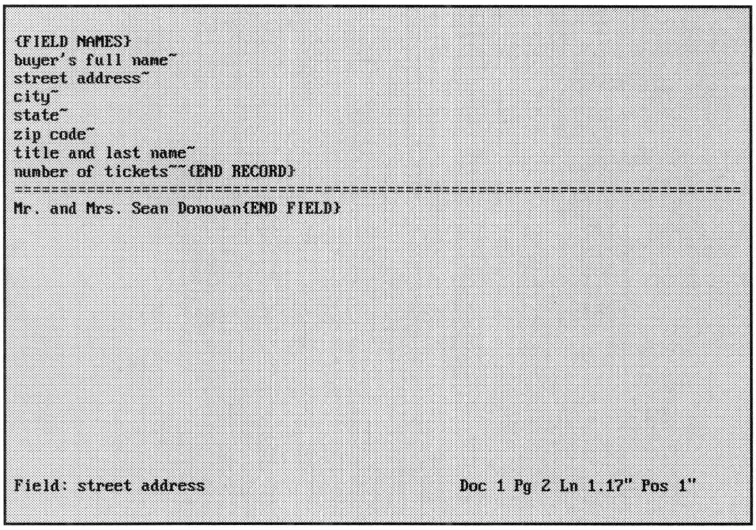

Figure 9-4:
First Record in Secondary File

Pressing [F9] inserts the {END FIELD} code and adds the next blank line. At the prompt of **Field 2:** on the status line,

3.....Repeat steps 1 and 2, typing the appropriate data as shown on the previous page, until you have entered all of the fields.

Be sure to enter the whole street address as 2 lines by pressing **[Enter]** after the first line and {END FIELD} **[F9]** only after the second line.

When the prompt for Field 8 appears,

4.....Press **[Shift]+[F9], 2** to insert the {END RECORD} code.

The prompts will start over again with Field 1 for the next record, as shown in Figure 9-5.

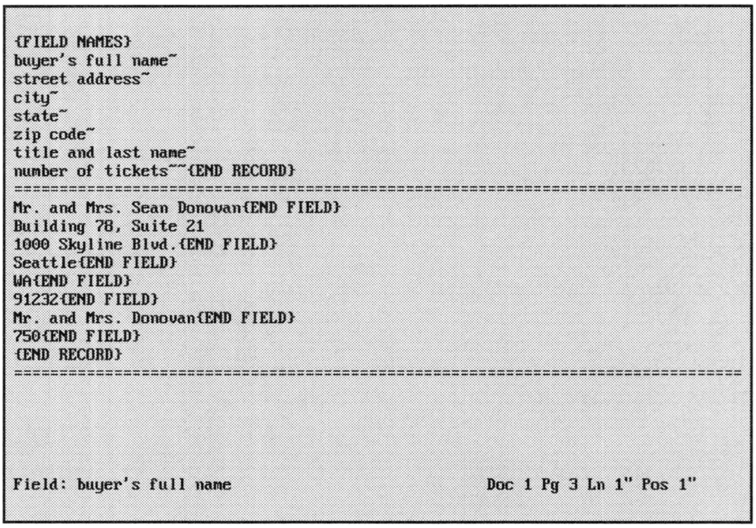

```
{FIELD NAMES}
buyer's full name~
street address~
city~
state~
zip code~
title and last name~
number of tickets~~{END RECORD}
================================================================================
Mr. and Mrs. Sean Donovan{END FIELD}
Building 78, Suite 21
1000 Skyline Blvd.{END FIELD}
Seattle{END FIELD}
WA{END FIELD}
91232{END FIELD}
Mr. and Mrs. Donovan{END FIELD}
750{END FIELD}
{END RECORD}
================================================================================

Field: buyer's full name                                Doc 1 Pg 3 Ln 1" Pos 1"
```

Figure 9-5: *Completed 1st Record in 2nd File*

Enter the following records into the file:

Mrs. Sandy Arnold
1946 Upper Crest Drive
Whersits
WA
94920
Mrs. Arnold
500

Mr. Ronald B. Jones
22505 Mtn. Top Road
Newberg
OR
97132
Mr. Jones
1,500

When you finish typing the secondary file names, save the file under the name of TICKETS. You must add the extension .SF after the file name to tell the computer that this file is a secodary file. To do so press **[F10]**. When the computer asks for the document's file name,

Type A:TICKETS.SF and press **[Enter]** to store the file on the data disk.

In specialized applications, it is a good idea to use the same first name for both the primary and secondary files, varying only the extensions .PF and

.SF. This way, you can tell at a glance when you look at the List Files screen that the two files belong together.

Clear the screen.

Creating Primary Files

The primary file contains the document that will become the customized form letter. The raw form letter must contain the codes instructing the computer to insert the appropriate data from the secondary file.

In the primary file, you can identify secondary file fields by name or by number. Because you have already established the specific data in the secondary file fields, you must use a numeric field designation or the name of the field to identify the correct data (field).

In this exercise, you will create the form letter shown in Figure 9-6. Clear the screen and position the cursor at the top of the screen. To create the primary file form letter,

> (today's date)
>
> (buyer's full name)
> (street address)
> (city, state zip)
>
> Dear (title and last name):
>
> Thank you for your generous purchase of (number of tickets) tickets to the Goodwill Games. We greatly appreciate your support and look forward to holding this international event in our city.
>
> Yours truly,
>
> Dan Miner

Figure 9-6: *Primary File Form Letter*

1.....Press **[Shift]+[F9]**
The following prompt will appear on the status line:
1 Field; **2 E**nd Record; **3 I**nput; **4 P**age Off; **5 N**ext Record; **6 M**ore: **0**

2.....Press **6** to go to the menu shown in Figure 9-7.
To insert today's date, move the cursor to {DATE} or

3.....Press **D [Enter]** and the code for the current date will appear at the position of the cursor. (The actual date will be inserted during the merge process.)
Create two blank lines. To insert the buyer's name,

4.....Press **[Shift]+[F9]**
From the following menu:
1 Field; **2 E**nd Record; **3 I**nput; **4 P**age Off; **5 N**ext Record; **6 M**ore: **0**

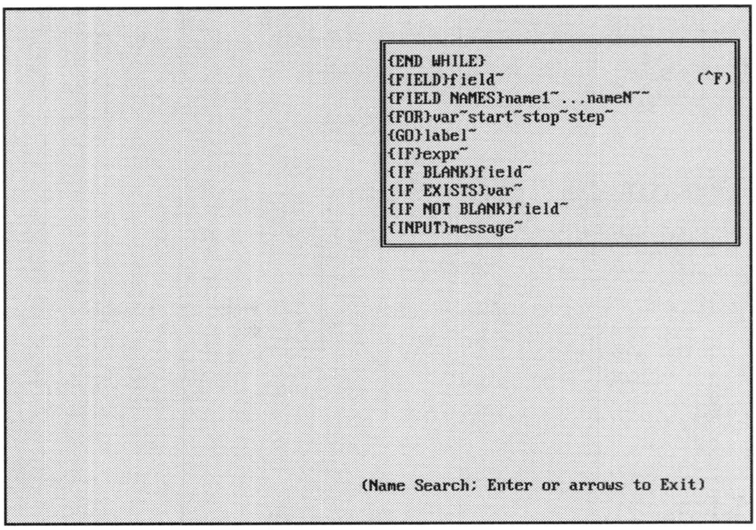

Figure 9-7:
Primary File Format Menu

5. . . . .Press **1**
The status line will request the field number. Type either the field name (buyer's full name) or the field number of the record, in this case **1**.
6. . . . .Press **1** for field number 1.
Do not press [Enter]! A tilde (~) has to be added to the entry to indicate to the computer that it is not a part of the text.
To complete the entry,
7. . . . .Press **[↓]** to position the field designation in the document where it belongs and add a tilde.
8. . . . .Press **[Enter]**
Repeat steps 4 through 8 to enter the coding for the street address.

To place the city, state, and ZIP code on the same line using their field names rather than their field numbers,

1. . . . .Press **[Shift]+[F9], 1** to select the field to enter.
To enter the field by its name,
2. . . . .Type **CITY [↓]**
To add the comma and space between the city and state,
3. . . . .Type **,** and press **[Space]**
To enter the state,
4. . . . .Press **[Shift]+[F9], 1**
5. . . . .Type **STATE** and press **[↓]**
Add two spaces after the code and,
6. . . . .Press **[Shift]+[F9], 1**
To enter the ZIP code,
7. . . . .Type **ZIP CODE** and press **[↓] [Enter]**

The line is now complete. Add a blank line before entering the text and code for the salutation. To enter the salutation,

1.....Type **Dear** and press **[Space]**
To select the title and last name field,
2.....Press **[Shift]+[F9], 1**
To enter the field number,
3.....Press **6 [↓] : [Enter]** and the salutation is complete.

Complete the rest of the letter as shown in Figure 9-6. Be sure to insert field 7 (number of tickets) with a space in front of and behind the {FIELD}7~ code. Save the letter using the file name TICKETS and the extension .PF for primary file. Clear the screen.

Merging

Now that you have created a primary file and a secondary file, you can merge the two files. When WordPerfect generates form letters, they will appear on screen with a hard page break separating them.

To merge the two files to produce the customized form letters,

1.....Press **[Ctrl]+[F9]**
When the following menu appears on the status line:
1 Merge; **2 S**ort; **3 C**onvert Old Merge Codes: **0**

2.....Press **1**
The following request will appear:
Primary file: (**List** Files)

3.....Type **A:TICKETS.PF** and press **[Enter]**
If you forget the file name, you can press List Files and then select the file. After you successfully identify the correct file, the following request will appear:
Secondary file: (**List** Files)

4.....Type **A:TICKETS.SF** and press **[Enter]**
The message * **Merging** * will briefly appear on the screen and then be replaced with the completed letter which includes the last record from the secondary file.

Position the cursor at the top of the file and use the [PgDn] key to scroll down through the letters to see if they are correct.

You can now print all of the letters or save them to a new file. You can merge the secondary file again with a different form letter (primary file), or use it to create envelopes or mailing labels from the names and addresses in the list.

Merging Without a Secondary File

Imagine a personnel office that sends two or three letters a day acknowledging resumes it has received. Because the variable data arrives daily, it is impossible to create a secondary file with all the names and addresses the office needs to send these letters. However, the office can set up a form letter thanking each applicant and letting them know their resume will be on file for six months. The office can then use this letter whenever it receives a resume. This method is also practical for creating frequently used forms such as memos.

Instead of typing names and addresses in a secondary file, create a form letter using codes that you will use when you type the variable data at the time of the merge; in other words, there is no secondary file. Note that you should use this method only if you do not need to save the variable data in a file for later use (that is, to send another letter to the same person).

In the following exercise, you will enter information from the keyboard to merge with the primary file. First, however, you will need to create a new coded version of the primary file TICKETS.PF as shown in Figure 9-8.

```
{DATE}

{INPUT}Type name(s) ~
{INPUT}Type address~
{INPUT}Type city, state and zip~

Dear {INPUT}Type appropriate greeting~:

Thank you for your generous purchase of {INPUT}Type the number~
tickets to the Goodwill Games. We greatly appreciate your support
and look forward to hosting this international event in our city.

Yours truly,

Dan Miner
```

Figure 9-8: *Coded Primary File*

Notice that {INPUT} codes have replaced the {FIELD} codes. When you execute the merge, the {INPUT} code forces the cursor to stop at that position and wait for you to enter data. For example, the first time the cursor stops, you will type the person's name. The second time, type the address. After you finish entering the address, press the Merge Return [F9] key and the cursor will move to the position of the next {INPUT} code, where you will type the salutation.

To begin, clear the screen and retrieve the A:TICKETS.PF file. Erase all of the field codes.

With the cursor at the position where the letter in Figure 9-6 had been (buyer's full name),

1.....Press **[Shift]+[F9]**
To select the INPUT code from the following menu:
1 Field; **2 E**nd Record; **3 I**nput; **4 P**age Off; **5 N**ext Record; **6 M**ore: **0**

2.....Press **3**
When the following prompt appears on the status line:
Enter Message:

3.....Type **Type name(s)** and press **[Enter] [Enter]**
The {INPUT} code and message will appear in the primary file form as shown in Figure 9-9.

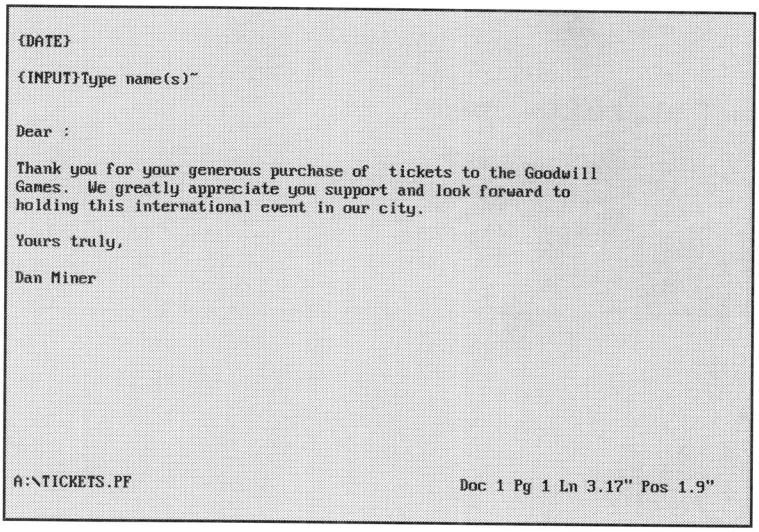

```
{DATE}

{INPUT}Type name(s)~


Dear :

Thank you for your generous purchase of  tickets to the Goodwill
Games.  We greatly appreciate you support and look forward to
holding this international event in our city.

Yours truly,

Dan Miner









A:\TICKETS.PF                              Doc 1 Pg 1 Ln 3.17" Pos 1.9"
```

Figure 9-9: *Beginning of Primary Form Letter*

4.....Repeat steps 1 through 3 until all fields have been replaced with an {INPUT} code and an appropriate message as shown in Figure 9-8.

Save the file under the new file name A:QUIKFORM.PF. Clear the screen. You are now ready to generate a form letter to be filled in as needed.

1.....Press **[Ctrl]+[F9]**
To start the merge process,

2.....Press **1**
When the following prompt appears:
Primary file: (**List** Files)

3.....Type **A:QUIKFORM.PF** and press **[Enter]**
If you forget the file name, you can press List Files and then select the file. After you successfully identify the correct file, the following request will appear:

Secondary file: (**List** Files)

4.....Press **[Enter]** to tell the computer that there is no secondary file to use. The message * **Merging** * will briefly appear on the status line, followed by the prompt **Type name(s)**.

5.....Type **Mr. Ronald B. Jones** and press **[F9]**
Do not press the [Enter] key at the end of the line. Use the [Enter] key when the INPUT entry requires more than one line. The [F9] key signals the computer that the particular entry is finished.

6.....Repeat step 5 for each of the {INPUT} entries in the form. When you have typed in the last entry, the last entry has been entered, the form will finish executing and then stop.

Print the letter. Clear the screen. If you wish to use the form again, repeat the procedure.

General Exercises

1. In order to practice merging two files and producing printed customized letters, create and save a primary file using the following form letter:
   Using the following record format, save the records in a secondary file:

Aromax and Family Corporation
1721 North Pierce Street
Grand Junction, CO 81501

(today's date)

(individual's name)
(position in company)
(room number)
(company office)

Dear (individual's name):

This will confirm your registration and attendance for the following class and dates:

(computer class)
(date of computer class)

If you are unable to attend, please notify us at least one week in advance.

Thank you.

(your name)
Training Administrator

Record Format	Record 1	Record 2
Individual's name	Rob Young	Torrey Matthew
Room number	Room A1	Room A1
Company Office	Headquarters	Headquarters
Computer class	DataPerfect	DataPerfect
Job title	VP-Production	Controller
Date of class	May 20, 1991	May 20, 1991
Record 3	Record 4	Record 5
Mark Ford	Rick Snook	Cathy Carrick
Room 711	Room 316	Room 515
Headquarters	General Office	Boulder Office
DataPerfect	WordPerfect	PlanPerfect
System Programmer	Tutorial Writer	District Manager
May 20, 1991	April 30, 1991	May 17, 1991

Save the final letters as PRAC7 on the student data disk.

2. Change the above form letter to one that you can fill in without using a secondary file at the time of the merge. Use the same company name and address records when you fill in the letter. Print the letters.
3. If you intend to go on to another set of exercises, clear the screen. If not, exit WordPerfect.

Course-Specific Exercises

Group A Accounting

1. Load WordPerfect if necessary. Create and save the appropriate files using the following form letter and records, and merge the files to create individually addressed letters.

WEE-LOAN-IT CREDIT UNION
Overdue Payment Notice

(Name)(date)
(Address)
(City, State, ZIP)

Dear Member:

Your account has been charged a **$5.00 OVERDUE PAYMENT FEE.**

Please remit the scheduled payment or contact our Member Services Department for special arrangements at: (800) 321-7654.

If there is a discrepancy, please bring or mail a copy of your documentation to the WEE-LOAN-IT CREDIT UNION Member Services Department.

Sincerely,

Member Services

Customer name and address file format		
Name	Helen Springer	Chris Combs
Address	25518 Springhill	1475 Barnes
City	Monroe	Salem
State	LA	MA
Zip	97456	97306

2. Change the primary file so that you can insert the variable data at the time of the merge. Use the same customer names and addresses.
3. If you intend to go on to another set of exercises, clear the screen. If not, exit Wordperfect.

Group B Marketing

1. Load WordPerfect if necessary. Create and save the appropriate files using the following form letter and records, and merge the files to create individually addressed letters.

CEDAR HOMES BY SMITH, JOHNSON, & JONES
Sawmill, Idaho - 88525
(date)

(Name)
(Address)
(City, State, ZIP)

Thank you for your request for information about the SMITH, JOHNSON, & JONES Cedar Log Homes.

Enclosed you will find our catalog with complete information regarding features, sizes, insulation (R-values) for all of our Cedar log homes.

We deliver to any building site within 1,000 miles of our factory here in Sawmill, Idaho.

If we can be of any further help, please call us toll-free at:

1-800-(765)-4321

Sincerely yours,

Herb Jones
Sales Vice-President

Customer name and address file format	Customer	Customer
Name	Daryl Meyer	Don Peters
Address	11320 Flavel	123 Park Ave
City	Fields	Chicago
State	OR	IL
Zip	97777	56789

2. Change the primary file so that you can insert the variable data at the time of the merge. Use the same customer names and addresses.
3. If you intend to go on to another set of exercises, clear the screen. If not, exit WordPerfect.

Group C Finance

1. Load WordPerfect if necessary. Create and save the appropriate files using the following form letter and records, and merge the files to create individually addressed letters.

No PAIN — No GAIN
Health Club

(First Last)(Date)
(Cust Acct #)
(Address)
(City, State, ZIP)

Dear (First):

Another year has passed and your membership to the **No PAIN — No GAIN Health Club** is about to expire.

We are sure that you will want to continue your membership. In the coming year, we will be adding a new advanced aerobics class and child-care facility. Even with these new features, the yearly membership will remain at last year's low price of $360.

Just stop by the Business Office or mail your check in the enclosed, self-addressed envelope. As the Nike slogan goes:

Just do it!

Sincerely,

Member Services

Customer name and <u>address file format</u>	<u>Customer</u>	<u>Customer</u>
First	Mark	Leslie
Last	Wheeler	Harmon
Address	3512 1st Ave	2801 SE 1st St
Company name	Boyd Coffee	(no company name)
City	Great Falls	Helena
State	MT	MT
ZIP	45633	45722
Cust Acct	# AB346	AC459

2. Change the primary file so that you can insert the variable data at the time of the merge. Use the same customer names and addresses.
3. If you intend to go on to another set of exercises, clear the screen. If not, exit WordPerfect.

Group D Production

1. Load WordPerfect if necessary. Create and save the appropriate files using the following form letter and records, and merge the files to create individually addressed letters.

> **Wee-Kan MaeKit PRODUCTS**
> **CUSTOMER ORDER CONFIRMATION**
>
> (Date)
>
> (Name)
> (Company)
> (Address)
> (City, State ZIP)
> (Customer acct no.)
>
> Dear Valued Customer:
>
> We are writing to confirm your recent order.
>
> We also want to assure you that we specialize in Just-In-Time delivery to meet your need date.
>
> If we can be of further service to you, please call:
>
> **1-800-123-4567**
>
> Sincerely,
> Customer Service

Customer name and address file format	Customer	Customer
Name	Tanya Colie	Landon Morse
Address	5524 Claude Ave.	524 Cranberry Ct. Suite 2
Company name	Hunky-Dory Inc.	(no company name)
City	Reedsport	Gresham
State	AZ	OR
Zip	85324	97003
Cust Acct No.	4356	6559

Customer	Customer	Customer
Agus Lukman	Kathy Becker	Craig Brodie
317 NE Alemendra St.	1705 SW 11th Ave.	4300 Maritime Way
Las Cruces News	Hit & Miss	Happy Campers Inc
Las Cruces	Laramie	Vancouver
NM	WY	WA
93505	56334	93001
2275	8402	5963

2. Change the primary file so that you can insert the variable data at the time of the merge. Use the same customer names and addresses.
3. Exit WordPerfect.

10

Tables and Spreadsheets

The objectives of this lesson are to

- Create a table
- Edit a table
- Perform mathematical computations in WordPerfect
- Create a spreadsheet in WordPerfect
- Define mathematical relationships
- Modify the mathematical table and recalculate

Creating Tables

A new feature in WordPerfect allows the user to create tables, and provides an easy method for organizing data in tabular form. It automatically enters tabs, as well as horizontal and vertical lines which can be edited from no lines to thick lines. This feature is especially useful for creating documents with data that must be organized in horizontal and vertical form.

The command **[Alt] + [F7]** activates the Table feature.

In this exercise you will create a table ten rows deep and four columns wide. You will use this form to record information on parking permits.

Load WordPerfect if necessary and position the cursor at the top left of the screen.

1.....Press **[Alt]+[F7]**
From the following menu:

1 Columns; **2 T**ables; **3 M**ath: **0**

2.....Press **2** to select Tables.
From the following menu:

Table: 1 Create; **2 E**dit: **0**

3.....Press **1** to select Create.
At the prompt

Number of Columns: 3

4.....Press **4 [Enter]**
At the prompt

Number of Rows: 1

5.....Press **10 [Enter]**
You will have a screen like the one shown in Figure 10-1.

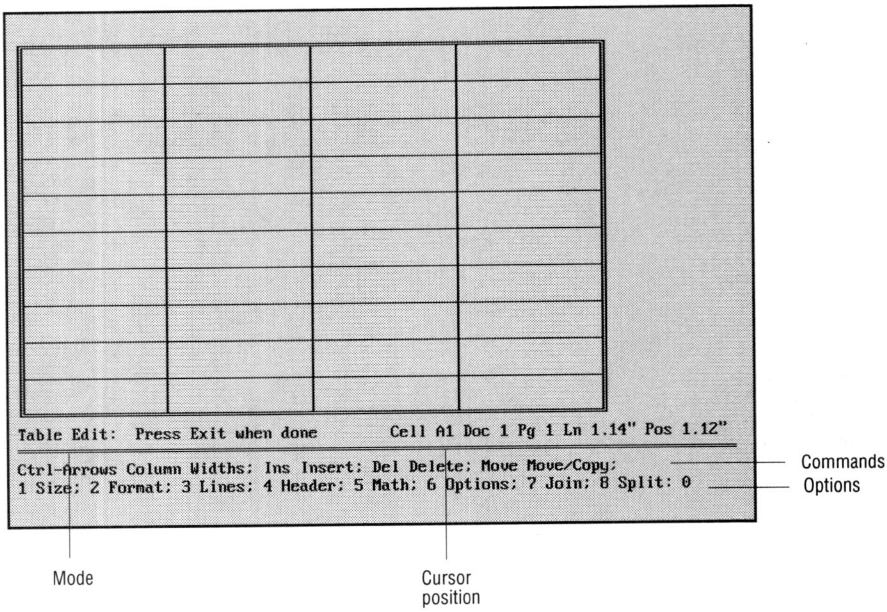

Figure 10-1: *A 10-row 4-column Table*

6.....Press **[F7]** to display the table only on the screen.

Each of the blocks in the table is uniquely identified by a combination of an alphabetic character and a number. The columns are labeled alphabetically left to right beginning with the letter A. The rows are numbered in consecutive order beginning with the top row, which is row 1. The intersection of a row and a column is known as a cell. The intersection of row 1 and column A is cell A1. All cells are identified by the column label and the row number.

After displaying the table on the screen, you can enter text material in each of the cells. Note that the cursor was automatically positioned in the upper left-hand corner of the table.

Entering Text in a Table

In this exercise, you will enter the following column headings in each of the identified cells:

Cell	**Column Heading**
A1	Student Name

B1	ID Number
C1	License Number
D1	Permit Number

NOTE: Do not use the [Enter] key when entering data into a table. Use only the cursor movement keys.

To enter the column headings, check the position of the cursor. With the cursor in cell A1,

1.....Type **Student Name**
To move to cell B1,
2.....Press **[→]**
Repeat steps 1 and 2 while typing in the appropriate column heading until you have entered all of the headings.

Follow the above procedure to enter the rest of the records.

Sollars, R.	989-66-5558	DSG 554 2501
Satter, J.	999-45-7685	AAL 747 2502
Tenkate, M.	463-43-5305	QQS 490 2503
DiFrancisco, M.	533-26-7723	GINVU2 2504

In the last entry, the student name "DiFrancisco, M." is too long for the cell. WordPerfect will attempt to solve the problem by using two lines for the name. However, if you want to keep the line height spacing even and maintain a uniform appearance for all entries, you should widen the column.

To widen the column, go to the Table Edit mode.

1.....Press **[Alt]+[F7]**
Move the cursor to the column to be widened and
2.....Press **[Ctrl]+[→]** once.

Widening the column one space was enough to keep all of the name "Di-Francisco, M." on one line. If one space had not been enough, you would need to repeat step 2.

3.....Press [F7] to exit Table Edit mode.

Inserting a Column

You have created columns for the student's name, ID number, license number, and permit number. Now you find that you need a column to enter the state from which the license plate comes. In this exercise, you will create a new column, labeled State, between the License Number and Permit Number columns.

To insert the new column, press **[Alt] + [F7]** to go to the Table Edit mode and position the cursor at the top of the column immediately to the right of the License Number column.

1.....Press **[Insert]**
From the following menu:
Insert: 1 Rows; **2 C**olumns: **0**

2.....Press **2**
To insert one column,
3.....Press **1 [Enter]**

In the resulting table, the new column is squeezed in and the heading for the Permit Number column is pinched. To improve the table's appearance, you can adjust the Permit Number column so that it has a two-line heading.

Move the cursor bar to cell C1 (which contains the heading for the License Number column) and

1.....Press **[Ctrl] + [←]** repeatedly until the column is adjusted for a two-line heading.
Move the cursor bar to cell E1 (which contains the heading for the Permit Number column) and
2.....Press **[Ctrl] + [→]** repeatedly until the column heading becomes a two-line heading as shown in Figure 10-2.

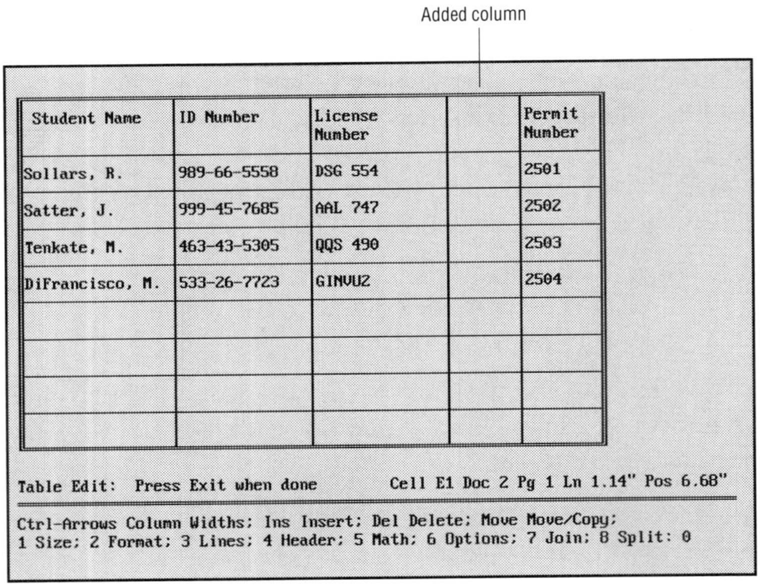

Figure 10-2: *Table with Entries & Added Column*

3.....Press **[F7]** to leave Table Edit mode.

Position the cursor in cell D1, at the top of the new column. To place the single line of a heading on the lowest line of a cell that can hold two lines,

1.....Press **[Enter]**
2.....Type **State**

This exercise demonstrates that text in a cell capable of holding more than one line always starts on the top line and only moves to lower lines when you press the [Enter] key or when there is no more space on the upper line. You saw a demonstration of this automatic shifting when you typed the name "DiFrancisco, M." in the table and the program moved part of the name to a second line.

Now change the position of the Student Name and ID Number column headings from the top line to the bottom line of the cell. Position the cursor on the "S" of "Student Name" and press [Enter]. Repeat this procedure for the ID Number heading. The column headings now occupy the second line of the cell.

To complete the table, enter the following state codes with the corresponding permit numbers:

State	Permit Number
CA	2501
OR	2502
WA	2503
NY	2504

Save the table as A:TABLE1 and clear the screen.

Sorting a Table

Sorting a table with column headings can be a little different from sorting a table with no headings. However, for predictable results in either case, use block sorting. Block sorting is especially useful when a table contains headings that you do not want to disturb.

Each set of entries containing information about a student is a record. The individual pieces of information, for example, the ID number are called fields. Each record in a table is treated as a single line and all the fields in a record remain with the record when you sort it. To see how sorting works, in this exercise you will alphabetize the names in the Student Name column.

Retrieve your A:TABLE1 file. Position the cursor on the "S" of "Sollars" in the first record.

1. . . . .Press **[Alt]+[F4]** or **[F12]** to start the blocking operation.
   Move the cursor down to highlight "DiFrancisco."
2. . . . .Press **[Ctrl]+[F9]** to start the Sort Table procedure as shown in Figure 10-3.
   From the menu on the Status line,
3. . . . .Press **3** to select the Keys option.

The Keys option allows you to identify key 1, the key you intend to use to sort the field. Key 2 is the next most important key, the key you will use to sort in the same field. The field must contain at least two characters or words separated by a comma, a space, a forward slash, or a hyphen if you use a second key. For example, the license plate numbers contain three alphabetic

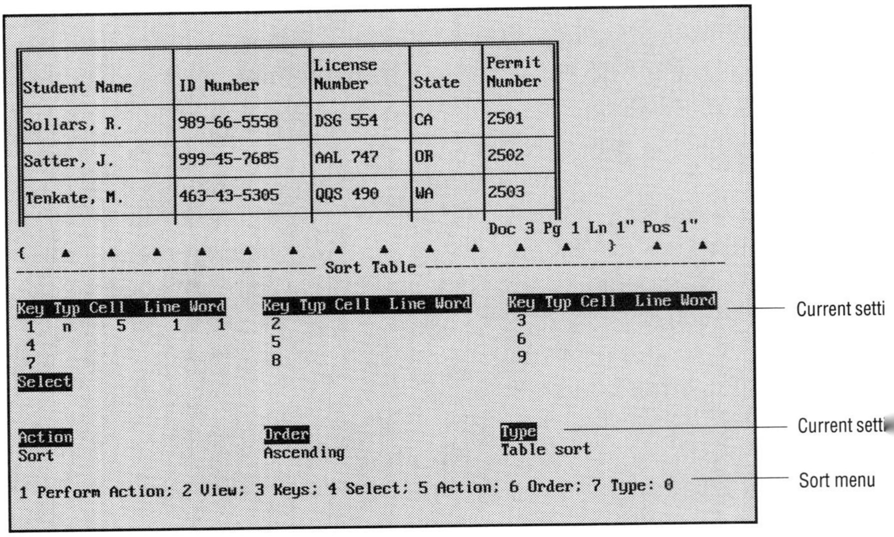

Figure 10-3: *Sort Table Procedure*

characters followed by a space and then three digits. You would use the second key to target the three digits.

To indicate that the first key is alphabetic, that is, that you want the program to sort the column alphabetically,

4. . . . .Press **A**
5. . . . .Press **1** for cell 1 in the record.
   With no other fields to set,
6. . . . .Press **[F7]** to stop the Key selection.
   To sort the names in the Student Name column,
7. . . . .Press **1**

The result will appear as in Figure 10-4. Note that the names are now in alphabetical order, and that the ID numbers, license numbers, etc. have also moved along with the names with which they belong.

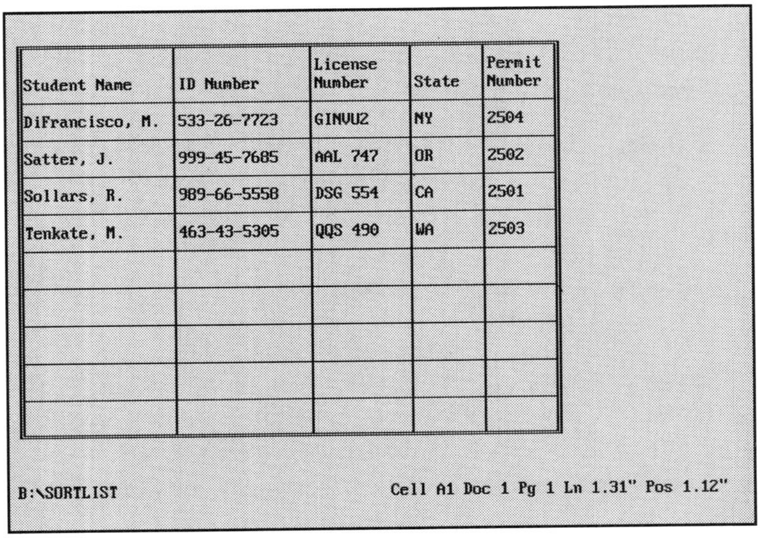

Figure 10-4: *Result of Alphabetical Sort*

Another option that you could have invoked is the Order option. This option allows you to change between ascending and descending order for the sorted records.

NOTE: Sorting can produce unpredictable results when all records do not have the same number of fields or are of different row heights.

Do not save the sorted file. Clear the screen.

Using the Math Command

WordPerfect allows you to perform certain useful mathematical computations. You can, for example, create a document with blank space that you will later fill in with appropriate numeric values to compute extensions for invoices. You can also retrieve an invoice form that only requires the insertion of a few numbers, thus speeding paperwork.

The Math command **[Alt]+[F7]** allows you to perform simple calculations within columns or tables of numeric data. Think of this command as a four-function calculator. You can use it in documents that have a standard format, such as invoices and expense reports. (If you need to work with complicated mathematical functions, use the Import command, which will be introduced in Lesson 11, to combine spreadsheet data with your word processing document.)

In this exercise, you will learn to create and edit a table with calculated columns, subtotals and a total. Creating and editing a math table involves five major steps:

1. Clearing WordPerfect's default tab settings and setting new tabs
2. Defining mathematical relationships among the columns
3. Turning the Math feature on and entering data in the table
4. Calculating the values in the table and turning Math off
5. Editing the table and performing the necessary recalculations

Center the following heading at the top of the page:

FULL-SERVICE COMPUTER COMPANY
Commission Report
For the Month of December 199X

You are now ready to perform the five steps outlined above, each of which in turn contains a sequence of steps. The steps to create the table to perform mathematical calculations for this example are as follows:

Clearing and Setting New Tab Stops

1.....Press **[Shift]+[F8], 1, 8** to select the tab-setting function.
With the cursor at the left margin,

2.....Press **[Ctrl]+[End]** to clear all of the tab stops.

Move the cursor to 1.5" and

3. . . . .Press **R** to set a right-justified tab stop.
Repeat steps 1 and 2 for 3.0", 4.5", 5.5" and 6.5".
4. . . . .Press **[F7] [F7]** to exit the Format command.

You will now begin to create the table shown in Figure 10-6.

1. . . . .Press **[Enter]** to insert a blank line.
2. . . . .Type **(your name)** and press **[Enter]**.
3. . . . .Press **[Shift] + _** (underscore) to create a line across the page.
4. . . . .Type **REVENUE**, press **[Tab]**, type **GROSS**, press **[Tab]**, type **RETURNS &**, press **[Tab]**, type **COMMISSION**, and press **[Enter]**.
5. . . . .Type **SOURCE**, press **[Tab]**, type **PROFIT**, press **[Tab]**, type **ALLOWANCES**, press **[Tab]**, type **BASIS**, press **[Tab]**, type **RATE**, press **[Tab]**, type **TOTAL** and press **[Enter]**.
6. . . . .Press **[Shift] + _** (underscore) to create another line across the page.

Defining Mathematical Relationships

To select the Define option of the Columns/Table command,

1. . . . .Press **[Alt]+[F7], 3, 3**

The Math Definition menu presents 24 columns, labeled A-X, across the screen as shown in Figure 10-5. Note that WordPerfect reserves the left-hand column in math tables for descriptive information. Thus, you will set up a GROSS PROFIT column in your document to correspond with column A. Use the arrow keys to move about in this menu.

```
Math Definition          Use arrow keys to position cursor

Columns                  A B C D E F G H I J K L M N O P Q R S T U V W X

Type                     2 2 2 2 2 2 2 2 2 2 2 2 2 2 2 2 2 2 2 2 2 2 2 2

Negative Numbers         ( ( ( ( ( ( ( ( ( ( ( ( ( ( ( ( ( ( ( ( ( ( ( (

Number of Digits to      2 2 2 2 2 2 2 2 2 2 2 2 2 2 2 2 2 2 2 2 2 2 2 2
  the Right (0-4)

Calculation   1
  Formulas    2
              3
              4

Type of Column:
     0 = Calculation     1 = Text      2 = Numeric     3 = Total

Negative Numbers
     ( = Parentheses (50.00)           - = Minus Sign  -50.00


Press Exit when done
```

Figure 10-5: *Mathematical Relationships Menu Mode*

Below the "Columns" heading on the menu is a "Type" heading. The four column types are

0 = Calculation
1 = Text
2 = Numeric
4 = Total
The default setting for all of the columns is **2**, Numeric.

Move the cursor to the 2 under the letter C in the table and

2.....Press **0** to change C to Column Type 0, Calculation. The cursor moves down automatically to the Calculation Formulas area.

3.....Type **A+B** to indicate that COMMISSION BASIS equals the sum of GROSS PROFIT and RETURNS & ALLOWANCES.

4.....Press **[Enter]** to stop the calculation formula.
Position the cursor on the 2 under the letter E.

5.....Press **0** to change the Column Type to Calculation.

6.....Type **C*D** to indicate that COMMISSION BASIS times RATE equals TOTAL.
Move the cursor to the "Number of Digits to the Right" row and position it on the 2 in column A.

7.....Press **0**
Change the readings in the "Number of Digits to the Right" row for columns B, C, and E in the same manner.

8.....Press **[Enter]** to exit the Define option.

Turning Math On and Entering Data

After completing the above steps, you will be returned to the Math prompts. You can now turn the Math feature on.

1.....Press **1** to turn Math on. A message in the lower left corner on the status line will indicate that you have turned the Math feature on.

2.....Type **Hardware** and press **[Tab]**

3.....Type **21,000** in the GROSS PROFIT column. You may type the comma in the number.

4.....Press **[Tab]** and type **(2,200)**. The parentheses indicate a negative amount in the RETURNS column.

5.....Press **[Tab]** An (!) appears on the screen. The exclamation point indicates that the COMMISSION column is a calculated column. Do not type anything here.

6.....Press **[Tab]** and type **.10** to indicate a 10 percent value in the RATE column.

7.....Press **[Tab]**. Another (!) appears in the TOTAL column.

8.....Press **[Enter]** to indicate the end of the present line.
Add the next two lines as shown in Figure 10-6 using the above procedure.
When you have entered the next two lines,

1.....Press **[Alt]+[F7], 3, 3** to go to the Math Definition menu. Change columns C and E to Column Type **2**.

```
              FULL-SERVICE COMPUTER COMPANY
                    Commission Report
             For the Month of December 199X

C. Sorenson
--------------------------------------------------------------------------
REVENUE   GROSS       RETURNS &      COMMISSION
SOURCE    PROFIT      ALLOWANCES          BASIS        RATE       TOTAL
--------------------------------------------------------------------------
Hardware  21000          (2200)               !         .10           !
Software   3600           (500)               !         .10           !
Consulting 5000              0                !         .50           !




Math                                         Doc 2 Pg 1 Ln 3" Pos 1"
```

Figure 10-6:
Spreadsheet

After changing the two columns,

2.....Press **[F7]**
3.....Press **1** to turn Math on.
4.....Press **[Enter]** to insert a blank line under the body of the table.
5.....Press **[Tab]** five times to move to the TOTAL column.
6.....Type **$+** to indicate that a subtotal is to be placed at this point.
7.....Press **[Enter]**

Calculating the Values

Now that you have created the spreadsheet table, it is time to calculate the values which will appear next to the (!) and (+) markers.

To perform the calculations,

1.....Press **[Alt]+[F7], 3, 4**
Check the values to make sure they are reasonable.

You have now created a simple math table.

Editing and Recalculating

To edit and recalculate, copy the spreadsheet starting with the cursor at the first letter of your name and place the copy below the current table.

You will use the second table to enter data for a second business associate, K. Trautmann. Replace your name in the second table with the new name, "K. Trautmann." Position the cursor at the "H" of "Hardware" in the second table, and perform the following steps to edit and recalculate the new:

1.....Press **[Alt]+[F7], 3, 1** to turn Math On.

Use the normal editing and cursor movement keys to change the numbers in the GROSS PROFIT and RETURNS columns to those given in Figure 10-7.

```
                    FULL-SERVICE COMPUTER COMPANY
                          Commission Report
                     For the Month of December 199X
C. Sorenson
----------------------------------------------------------------------------
REVENUE   GROSS        RETURNS &        COMMISSION
SOURCE    PROFIT      ALLOWANCES             BASIS        RATE        TOTAL
----------------------------------------------------------------------------
Hardware 21,000          (2,200)          18,800!          .10   1,880!
Software  3,600            (500)           3,100!          .10     310!
Consulting5,000                0           5,000!          .50   2,500!

                                                                $4,690+
K. Trautmann
----------------------------------------------------------------------------
REVENUE   GROSS        RETURNS &        COMMISSION
SOURCE    PROFIT      ALLOWANCES             BASIS        RATE        TOTAL
----------------------------------------------------------------------------
Hardware 18,600          (1,500)          18,800!          .10   1,880!
Software  4,700            (600)           3,100!          .10     310!
Consulting3,500                0           5,000!          .50   2,500!

                                                                $4,690+
Align char = . Typeover  Math                   Doc 2 Pg 1 Ln 4.33" Pos 3.83"
```

Figure 10-7: *Enlarged Spreadsheet*

Insert a blank line under the subtotal value in the second table. To calculate a total of the subtotals,

2. . . . .Press **[Tab]** five times.
3. . . . .Type **$=** and press **[Enter]** in the TOTALS column.
4. . . . .Press **[Alt]+[F7], 3, 4** to do the recalculation.
5. . . . .Press **[Alt]+[F7], 3, 2** to turn Math off.

Your WordPerfect spreadsheet is now complete. Save the file as WP_SS and clear the screen.

General Exercises

1. Load WordPerfect if necessary. Retrieve your A:TABLE1 file.
   A. Add the following records to the table:

Curran, R.	543-66-3862	AAL 767	OR	2505
Bond, G.	543-45-9071	SA 007	OR	2506

   B. Sort the table alphabetically by student name.
   C. Sort the table in descending order by ID number.
   D. Sort the table in ascending order by license number with one key for the alphabetical characters and another for the digits.
   E. Sort the table in alphabetical order by state.
   F. Sort the table in ascending order by permit number.
2. Insert a column between the Student Name and ID Number columns. Label the new column Year. Make column adjustments to retain a single line per record. Use left and right margin settings of 1 inch.

3. If you intend to go on to another set of exercises, clear the screen. If not, exit WordPerfect.

Course-Specific Exercises

Group A Accounting

1. Load WordPerfect if necessary. Create a spreadsheet to perform the following aging of accounts.

AGING OF ACCOUNTS						
Name	Amount	0-30 Days	31-60 Days	61-90 Days	Over 90 Days	Total
Robb, L	$100.00	$50.00	$0.00	$0.00	$10.00	$160.00
Ford, B	$200.00	$25.00	$35.00	$45.00	$0.00	$305.00
Klein, R	$300.00	$0.00	$50.00	$0.00	$25.00	$375.00
Kromm, S	$150.00	$100.00	$100.00	$0.00	$0.00	$350.00
Seitz, T	$50.00	$50.00	$0.00	$0.00	$0.00	$100.00
TOTAL						

2. If you intend to go on to another set of exercises, clear the screen. If not, exit WordPerfect.

Group B Marketing

1. Load WordPerfect if necessary. Create a spreadsheet to compute the variance between the planned amount and the actual amount.
   Var = Planned - Actual

YEAR	Planned	Actual	Var.
SALES	250.00	300.00	
FC	75.00	82.50	
VC	150.00	143.00	
NET INC	15.00	20.70	
DIVIDENDS	7.50	10.35	
ASSETS	200.00	240.00	

2. If you intend to go on to another set of exercises, clear the screen. If not, exit WordPerfect.

Group C Finance

1. Load WordPerfect if necessary. Prepare a spreadsheet to compute the appropriate totals and subtotals for the quarterly Cash Flow Report.

Artronics Company Cash Flow Report				
	January	February	March	Qtr
RECEIPTS:				
Receipts from Cash Sales	97800	98400	99500	
Other Cash Receipts	2400	2700	2300	
Total Cash Receipts	100200	101100	101800	
Sub Total:				
PAYMENTS:				
Salaries	21304	21304	21304	
Wages	31070	31070	31070	
Payroll Taxes	5731	5731	5731	
Rent	6000	6000	6000	
Advertising	4000	4000	6000	
Sub Total:				
TOTAL				

2. If you intend to go on to another set of exercises, clear the screen. If not, exit WordPerfect.

Group D Production

1. Load WordPerfect if necessary. Create a spreadsheet to total the following inventory investment for a manufacturer of athletic shoes.

Type of Shoe	Units	Cost per Unit	Total Investment
Basketball	400	85.00	
Football	550	59.00	
Soccer	1000	45.00	
Baseball	600	55.00	
Track	800	39.00	
Golf	1250	89.00	
Tennis	300	65.00	
Walking	750	29.00	

2. Exit WordPerfect.

11

Importing Spreadsheets

The objectives of this lesson are to

- Import a spreadsheet
- Display the spreadsheet as a table or text
- Edit the imported spreadsheet
- Provide for updating of an imported spreadsheet

Using Spreadsheets

Spreadsheet applications programs are powerful tools for performing mathematical computations and are used to create all types of mathematical and statistical reports. The computational capabilities of spreadsheet programs far exceed the capabilities of word processing programs. Therefore, the ability to import and link spreadsheets is a useful feature in a word processing program.

WordPerfect 5.1 can import a spreadsheet from Lotus 1-2-3 (versions 1.0 to 2.2), Microsoft Excel (version 2.0), and PlanPerfect (versions 3.0 to 5.0). You can also import version 3.0 of Lotus 1-2-3 if the .WK3 format is translated to a .WK1 format. You must retrieve this translated file into Lotus 1-2-3 version 3.0 and then save it before WordPerfect can import it. WordPerfect 5.1 can also import the VP Planner Plus spreadsheet.

Importing a Spreadsheet

WordPerfect 5.1 provides commands that allow you to import the results of spreadsheet processing and combine them with word processing to create superior documents. In addition, WordPerfect can provide a link to the imported spreadsheet to supply updated material from the spreadsheet. You can import a spreadsheet that you intend to use only once, or you can link the spreadsheet to a word-processed document to reflect changes made in the spreadsheet. The command **[Ctrl] + [F5],5** allows you to import an existing spreadsheet into a WordPerfect document.

NOTE: When you use the Import option,* [Ctrl] + [F5],5*, you must have an already existing spreadsheet. However, if you use the Link option, you do not need to have an already existing spreadsheet.

The steps for importing a spreadsheet into WordPerfect are straightforward and logical. In the following exercise, you will import a previously created Lotus 1-2-3 version 2.2 spreadsheet whose file name is FULLDEAL.WK1 from your student data disk. (In this exercise, only the spreadsheet will be displayed.)

Load WordPerfect, if necessary.

1. . . . .Press **[Ctrl]+[F5]**, **5** to select the TextIn/Out mode and the Spreadsheet option.
   To import a spreadsheet into the WordPerfect document one time only,
2. . . . .Press **1**
   To select the Filename option,
3. . . . .Press **1**
   To import the spreadsheet file from the student data disk,
4. . . . .Type **A:FULLDEAL.WK1** and press **[Enter]**
   (Another way to select the desired file is to use the List Files **[F5]** key to retrieve the file.)
5. . . . .Press **2** to identify the block of cells in the spreadsheet that you want to import.
   If you press the [Enter] key without typing new range values, you will retrieve the entire spreadsheet.
6. . . . .Press **[Enter]** to retrieve the entire spreadsheet.
   To select the spreadsheet in table format,
7. . . . .Press **3**, **1**
   The table format in the WordPerfect document uses solid lines to indicate rows and columns.
8. . . . .Press **4**

The spreadsheet is now placed in the WordPerfect document in table form as shown in Figure 11-1.

After the computer places the spreadsheet in the WordPerfect document, you can edit the spreadsheet.

Editing a Spreadsheet

You can import a spreadsheet in one of two ways: as a table, as in the above exercise, or as text.

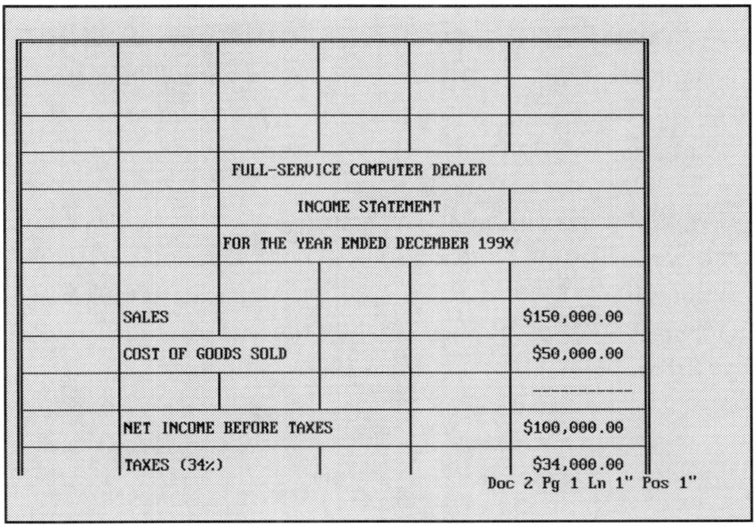

Figure 11-1: *Imported Spreadsheet as a Table*

If you import a spreadsheet as text, you can use the normal text-editing procedures to edit it. However, no matter how simple the change you intend to make, do not attempt to edit the spreadsheet in text form without first using Reveal Codes! If the cursor's position on the screen lies between codes, the desired change may not occur. Using Reveal Codes will show you the cursor's position with respect to codes. To go to Table Edit mode, use the command **[Alt]** + **[F7]**. To leave, press the Exit **[F7]** key.

After it imports the FULLDEAL.WK1 file in table form, the computer briefly displays a warning message indicating that the spreadsheet extends beyond the current margins. If you examine the form, you will find that you can make adjustments to bring the spreadsheet within the current margins. Three immediate solutions are to

1. Change the margin settings. (You must change them before importing the spreadsheet. See the section on Pitch and Points below.)
2. Delete Column A, which does not contain any data.
3. Change the width of a column that contains no data.

The easiest method of editing the spreadsheet is with the cursor inside the boundaries of the table. Position the cursor within the table's boundaries and

1. . . . . Press **[Alt]+[F7]**

   The computer will go immediately to the Table Edit mode, highlighting the cell in which the cursor was positioned before going to the Table Edit mode.

   If the highlighted cell is not the cell, column, or row you want to edit, move the cursor to the correct position.

   To leave the Table Edit mode and return to the word document,

2. . . . . Press **[F7]**

Adding and Deleting Columns and Rows

One way of adjusting the FULLDEAL.WK1 spreadsheet to fit between the margins of the document into which it was imported is to delete a column or columns.

Use the **[Alt] + [F7]** command to go to the Table Edit mode and position the cursor in column A. The status line, as shown in Figure 11-2, is now above the double line at the bottom of the screen. The two lines of information at the bottom of the screen indicate the options which are available for you to use while in Table Edit mode.

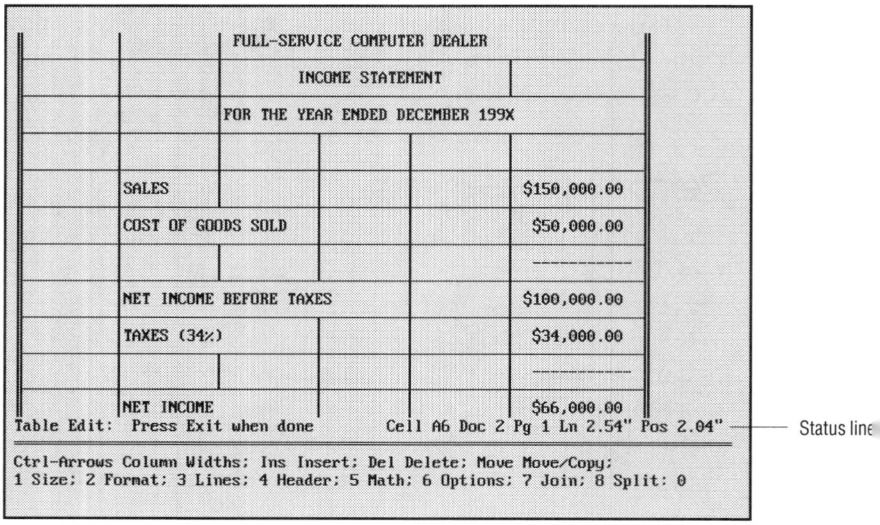

Figure 11-2: *Imported Spreadsheet in Table Edit*

In the Table Edit mode, the status line contains three pieces of information not normally given in the status line. First, it lets you know in bright characters that you are now in the Table Edit mode. Second, it tells you to press the Exit [F7] key to return to the word document. Third, it gives the cell address—its location by column and row—of the cell where the cursor is currently located.

The top line of the two lines below the status line indicates that you can use the **[Delete]** key to remove columns and rows. In this exercise, you will delete the current column A. Go to the Table Edit mode and position the cursor in column A.

1. . . . .Press **[Delete]**

   When the following prompt appears:

   Delete: 1 Rows; **2 C**olumns: **0**

2. . . . .Press **2**

   The prompt becomes

   Number of Columns: 1

Since you intend to delete only one column,

3.....Press **[Enter]**

The column is now deleted. If you want to delete more than one column, the computer will remove the column where the cursor is positioned and then those to its right.

To leave Table Edit mode,

4.....Press **[F7]**

You could just as easily have deleted rows instead of columns. When you want to remove rows, the computer will first remove the row beginning with the cursor position and then move downward.

To add columns or rows, use the **[Insert]** key and follow the prompts. The computer adds rows above the position of the cursor, and adds columns to the left of the cursor.

Restoring Deletions

You can restore deleted rows and columns to the document by using the Cancel **[F1]** key. The procedure is similar to the one you learned for restoring text in Lesson 3.

Assume you deleted too many rows from your table. In this exercise, you will reverse the deletion to restore four rows. Using the procedure given above for deleting rows, go to the Table Edit mode and position the cursor bar in cell A1.

To remove four rows,

1.....Press **[Delete], 1, 4, [Enter]**

When you examine the table, you find that the first line of the heading is missing. With the cursor bar in the new cell A1,

2.....Press **[F1]**

When the following menu appears:

Undelete Row(s)? No (**Y**es)

3.....Press **Y** to restore the 4 rows.

Follow the same procedure to restore columns.

NOTE: The computer stores the last three deletions in memory. If you do not notice a deletion error immediately, but do catch it before you have made three more deletions, you can restore the rows or columns. If you are using the command [Shift] + [F3] to switch between documents, WordPerfect keeps separate track of the last three deletions for each document.

Changing Pitch or Points

To reduce the width of the imported spreadsheet, you may opt to change the document's pitch, which is the number of characters per inch for the font. You might also choose to change to a smaller font, which is expressed in points. If you see the brief message,

WARNING Table extends beyond right margin

on the status line, you might solve the problem by reducing the font size or changing the pitch to allow additional characters to the inch.

You must change the pitch or point size before you import the spreadsheet. Because you have already imported the spreadsheet, you should now erase it from the document by using Reveal Codes. Choose a smaller font, and then import the spreadsheet again. (If you decide to change the margins to accommodate the too-wide table, you must use the same procedure if this change is to be effective.)

Changing Column Widths

You can widen or narrow the width of a column by using **[Ctrl]** plus a **[→]** or **[←]** cursor movement key. If a table fills the page, margin to margin, then widening a column will cause the other columns to become narrower, and making one column narrower will widen the others. By default, a table's left border is always positioned at the left margin of the page.

In this exercise, you will move the right column double line to approximately seven inches:

1.....Press **[Alt] + [F7]** to go to the Table Edit mode.
Position the cursor in column E and
2.....Press **[Ctrl]** and strike **[→]** until the right edge of the spreadsheet is changed to approximately seven inches.

To narrow a column, use the [Ctrl] key plus the **[←]** key.

You can change the height of a single row only by using the Format option in the Table Edit mode. The relative differences in row height are visible only in the View option of the Print command or the actual printed copy.

Moving or Copying Cells

The procedure for moving or copying cells in the Table Edit mode is similar to the use of the Move or Copy commands for editing regular text. In both situations you use the Block command **[Alt] + [F4]** or **[F12]** followed by the keystroke combinations for moving or copying text.

In this exercise, you will move the text material up three rows. Go to the Table Edit mode, if not there already, and position the cursor in cell A4.

1.....Press **[Alt]+[F4]** or **[F12]** to invoke the blocking function.
Move the cursor to cell E15 and
2.....Press **[Ctrl]+[F4]** to activate the Move command.
From the menu on the status line,

3.....Press **1, 1** to cut the blocked material in preparation to pasting it at the top of the form.
Position the cursor in cell A1 and

4.....Press **[Enter]**
The text material reappears in its new position. The 3 blank rows are now at the bottom of the table.

As a follow-up exercise, delete the three blank rows at the bottom of the table.

Joining Cells

One of the Table Edit mode's features allows you to join cells together to create the appearance of one cell. This procedure lends itself to changing the appearance of the top three lines that identify the spreadsheet. Figure 11-3 shows that the spreadsheet's heading is somewhat off-center because of the cell divisions. You can change the heading's appearance by deleting these cell divisions.

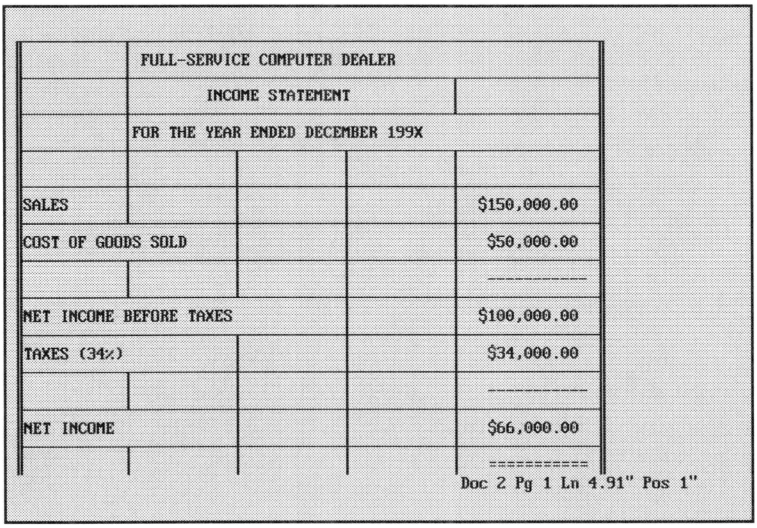

Figure 11-3: *Cell Arrangement Before Joining*

In the following exercise, you will change the top three lines and five columns so that they appear as one cell. A thick solid line is to separate the heading from the body of the spreadsheet. In a later exercise, you will center the heading.

The procedure for joining cells provides one method for eliminating the lines, and allows you to create one cell from the three rows and five columns.

Go to the Table Edit mode and position the cursor in cell A1, if not there already.

1.....Press **[Alt]+[F4]** or **[F12]**

Move the cursor bar to cell B3. Note that in this table, cell B3 extends to the right-hand border.

To join the highlighted rows and columns together as one cell,

2. . . . .Press **7**

In response to the prompt

Join cells? No (**Y**es)

3. . . . .Press **Y**

You should have a screen like the one shown in Figure 11-4.

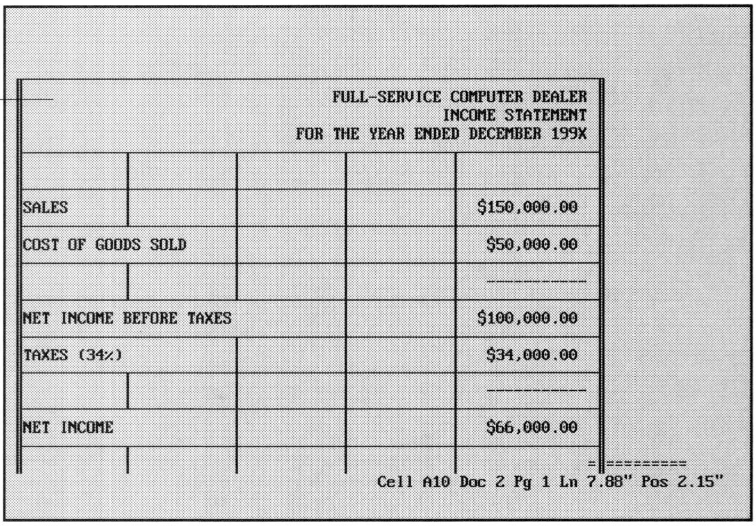

Figure 11-4: *Result of 3 Rows and Columns*

Now that the rows and columns are joined, you can change the line separating the heading from the body of the table. Stay in the Table Edit mode and position the cursor bar in cell A1, if not there already. (A1 is now a very large cell.)

1. . . . .Press **3** to select the Lines option.

The resulting menu tells you that there are a number of changes you can make in the cell. To change the bottom line of the cell,

2. . . . .Press **4**

To choose the Thick Line option from the menu,

3. . . . .Press **6**

4. . . . .Press **[F7]** to return to the normal screen edit mode.

5. . . . .Use the Reveal Codes command **[Alt] + [F3]** to delete the spaces to the left of each line in the heading, if there are any.

The heading will remain at the right edge of the table because the cell is right-justified.

Changing the Justification

When you import a spreadsheet, it may enter WordPerfect without the same exact positioning that it had in the spreadsheet program. If after you import the spreadsheet you want to change the justification of the material within the cells, the Table Edit mode allows you to make these changes.

In the FULLDEAL spreadsheet you imported, the spreadsheet titles are currently right-justified. Because you joined the cells in the previous exercise, the titles now occupy a single cell.

In this exercise, you will center the contents of cell A1. Go to the Table Edit mode and position the cursor on cell A1, if not there already.

1.....Press **2** to select the Format option.
2.....Press **1** to select the option that allows you to modify a single cell.
3.....Press **3** to inform the Table Editor you want to justify the cell.
From the menu that appears,
4.....Press **2** to select the Center option.

You have now centered the contents of the cell, which appear as in Figure 11-5, and the computer returns to the beginning of the Table Edit mode.

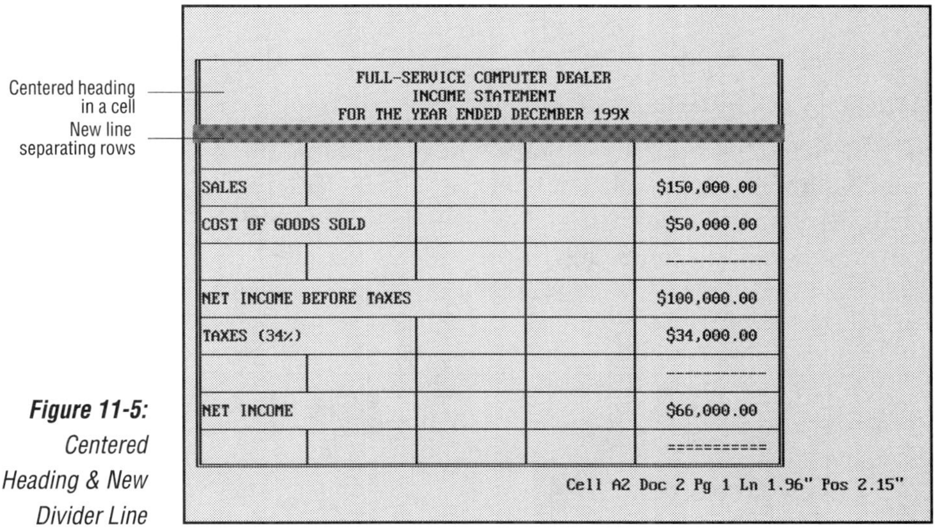

Figure 11-5: *Centered Heading & New Divider Line*

You can justify any cell, or you can justify an entire spreadsheet column by selecting option **2** in step **2** of the above justification procedure.

Positioning the Table

At this point the table is not the same size it was when you imported it. You have removed a column, and adjusted the column width. Within the options of the Table Edit mode, you can position the resulting table against the right or left margins, or center it, or widen it automatically to extend from the left margin to the right margin. A fifth option allows you to position the table at a certain location on the page. However, one disadvantage of this last option is that you will be unable to reposition the table if you decide to adjust surrounding material.

In this exercise, you will widen the table to fit between the margins.

Go to the Table Edit mode, if not there already, and

1.....Press **6** to select Options.
   To choose the Position of Table option from the menu displayed on the screen,
2.....Press **3**
   To choose the option that automatically widens the table so that it extends from left margin to right margin,
3.....Press **4**
   In the menu displayed on the screen, the Position of Table option now reads Full.
   To return to the Table Edit mode,
4.....Press **[F7]**
5.....Press **[F7]** again to leave Table Edit mode.
6.....Press **[F7], N, N,** to clear the screen.

Linking a Spreadsheet

The difference between importing a spreadsheet into the WordPerfect document and linking a spreadsheet with the WordPerfect document is that linking allows you to update material whenever you retrieve the WordPerfect document. Linking can produce a code to retrieve a spreadsheet that you intend to construct at a later time but that does not yet exist.

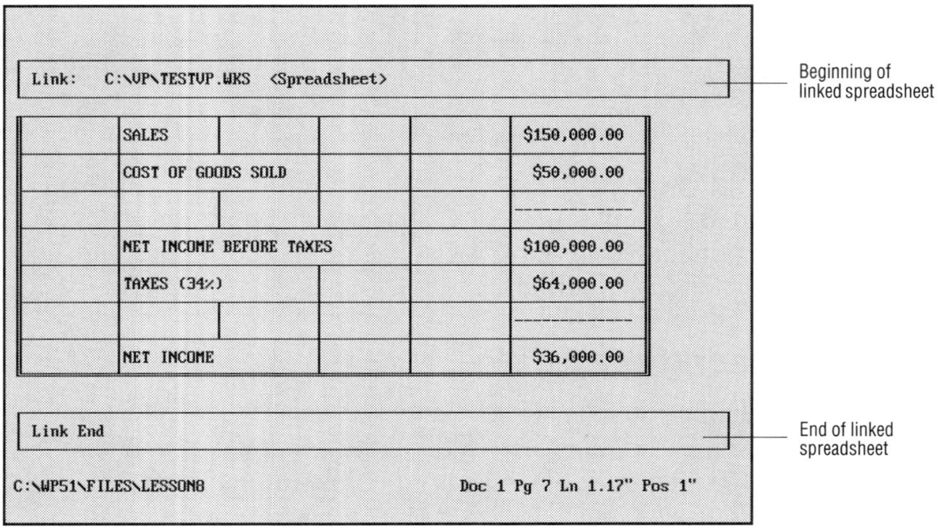

Figure 11-6: *Linked Spreadsheet Comment Boxes*

When you create a link between the WordPerfect document and the spreadsheet program, a box on the screen indicates the beginning of the spreadsheet and another box indicates the end as shown in Figure 11-6. Neither of the two comment boxes is ever printed, nor will the link codes be displayed in the normal screen editing mode.

The following exercise will take you through the procedure for importing and linking a spreadsheet. You will import a spreadsheet named TESTVP.WKS, which is stored on your student data disk. Clear the screen, if it is not already clear.

1.....Press **[Ctrl]+[F5], 5** to select the TextIn/Out mode and the Spreadsheet option.
To select the option that creates a link between the spreadsheet and the WordPerfect document,

2.....Press **2**
To select the spreadsheet that you intend to link with the WordPerfect document,

3.....Press **1**

4.....Type **A:TESTVP.WKS** and press **[Enter]**

Another method available for selecting a file is to use the List Files command **[F5], 1** to retrieve the desired file.

After you have specified the file name, you must indicate the range of cells to be imported.

5.....Press **2**

You can type in the identification of a beginning and ending cell if you do not want to import the entire spreadsheet. If you press the [Enter] key without typing new range values, the entire spreadsheet is retrieved.

To retrieve the entire spreadsheet,

6.....Press **[Enter]**
To select a table format for the spreadsheet, which in the WordPerfect document will have solid lines to indicate rows and columns,

7.....Press **3, 1**

8.....Press **4**

The spreadsheet is now placed in the WordPerfect document in table form. You can, if you wish, edit the structure by going to the Table Edit mode.

9.....Press **[F7] N, N,** to clear the screen.

Using the Link Options

WordPerfect provides three link options:

1 Update on Retrieve Y/N
2 Show Link Codes Y/N

3 Update All Links

You get to these link options by pressing **[Ctrl] + [F5], 5, 4**.

The first link option offers you a simple yes or no choice, asking if you want to update the imported spreadsheet upon retrieval of the WordPerfect document. If you set this option to NO, you essentially retain manual control, which allows you to update the spreadsheet at your convenience.

Using the second option to not show the link codes might be problematical. Without the comment boxes to indicate the links between the spreadsheet and the word document, you may not be able to tell the difference between an imported spreadsheet and a linked one simply by viewing the screen.

The third option gives you manual control to update the linked spreadsheets when you set the first option to NO. You choose the third option by pressing **3**.

Note: ***Any editing of the linked spreadsheet, such as the addition or deletion of columns and rows in the Table Edit mode, will be lost when you retrieve or update the WordPerfect document.***

General Exercises

1. Clear the screen and set the left margin to 1.5 inches and the right margin to 1.0 inch. Retrieve the spreadsheet file A:A&L.WK1 from your student data disk.
   A. Delete all rows below the Total Assets row.
   B. Join columns A and B.
   C. Delete the top row of dashes.
   D. Join the top row of cells.
   E. Join the second row of cells.
   F. Adjust the width of spreadsheet to fit between the margins.
   G. Join the top two rows.
   H. Center the spreadsheet heading.
   I. Print the document.
2. Clear the screen without saving the above changes and retrieve the spreadsheet file A:A&L.WK1 again. Erase the Asset section rows.
3. If you intend to go on to another set of exercises, clear the screen. If not, exit WordPerfect.

Course-Specific Exercises

Group A Accounting

1. Load WordPerfect if necessary. Set the margins to 1 inch on the right and the left. Change the base font to as small a pitch as possible (16.66 or

smaller). Import the ACCTGSS.WK1 spreadsheet file from your student data disk.

A. Delete the top two rows.

B. Delete row 3.

C. Expand column A.

D. Delete column B.

E. Delete all columns to the right of the Total column.

F. Adjust all columns to fit the spreadsheet between the margins.

G. Join the cells of column A and center the heading.

H. Join the cells of column B and center the heading.

I. Print the document.

2. Clear the screen without saving the above changes. Using the margin and font settings of Problem 1, link the ACCTGSS.WK1 spreadsheet file. Import only cells A3 through F30.

A. Insert a column between columns E and F.

B. Delete column F.

C. Label the new column "Total" on the same line with the "months" label.

D. Expand column A.

E. Delete column B.

F. Do parts G, H, and I of Problem 1.

3. If you intend to go on to another set of problems, clear the screen. If not, exit WordPerfect.

Group B Marketing

1. Load WordPerfect if necessary. Set the margins to 1 inch on the right and the left. With the base font set at 10-pitch, import the MRKTGSS1.WK1 spreadsheet file from your student data disk.

A. Examine the headings and spacing of the worksheet. Delete the spreadsheet and change the base font to as small a pitch as possible (16.66 or smaller). Retrieve the MRKTGSS1.WK1 spreadsheet file.

B. Delete column C (Population).

C. Delete the row of double dashes.

D. Join the cells for each column heading.

E. Change the column heading "Name" to "City and State" and center the new heading.

F. Adjust the spreadsheet to fit between the margins by changing to three-line headings where possible and reducing the column width.

G. Check the document using the View option of the Print command.

H. Print the document.

2. Clear the screen without saving the above changes. Import cells A1 through D16 from the MRKTGSS1.WK1 file.
   A. Insert a blank column at the extreme right of the spreadsheet. (Move column E to column D.)
   B. Set column E to three decimal places by pressing 2, 2, 4, 3 [Enter] while in Table Edit mode.
   C. Compute the percentage of population with four or more years of college for each city by pressing 5, 2, (D7/C7)*100 [Enter] with the cursor in cell E7.
   D. Copy the above formula into all cells of column E below cell E7.
   E. Change the lines between column D and E to a single line.
   F. Print the document.
3. If you intend to go on to another set of exercises, clear the screen. If not, exit WordPerfect.

Group C Finance

1. Load WordPerfect if necessary. Set the margins to 1 inch on the right and the left. With the base font at 10-pitch, import the LCHEEL.WK1 spreadsheet file from your student data disk.
   A. Try to fit the spreadsheet between the margins. If it does not fit, erase the imported spreadsheet and choose a smaller-pitch font.
   B. Delete column B.
   C. Adjust all the columns to fit the spreadsheet between the margins.
   D. Join the cells for each column heading.
   E. Delete the row of double dashes.
   F. Move the headings to the bottom of the cell and center them.
   G. Change the Interest Percentage from 10 to 9.75.
   H. Change the Mortgage Cancellation Insurance from 0 to .2%.
   I. Add a row at the top of the table for a heading. Join the cells to form one cell.
   J. Change the bottom line of the joined cell to a thick line.
   K. Center the heading S & M Check Register.
   L. Delete all unnecessary rows in the spreadsheet.
2. With the left and right margins set at 1 inch, create a link between the spreadsheet and LCHEEL.WK1.
   A. Repeat all of the exercises in Problem 1.
   B. What happens to the edited linked spreadsheet if you choose to execute option 3 (Update All Links) of the spreadsheet link options? Access these options by pressing ([Ctrl]+[F5],5,4).
3. If you intend to go on to another set of exercises, clear the screen. If not, exit WordPerfect.

Group D Production

1. Load WordPerfect if necessary. Import the spreadsheet PRODSHOE.WK1 from your student data disk. With a pitch of 10, fit the spreadsheet between left and right margins set at 1 inch. As a last resort, abbreviate words.
   A. Add a column between columns B and C. Give the new column the heading COLOR. Add the following text to the COLOR column:

	COLOR
Basketball	White
Football	Black
Soccer	Black/white
Baseball	Black
Track	White
Walking	White/red

   B. Join the cells for each column heading.
   C. Left justify the SHOES and STYLE column headings. Center all other headings.
   D. Add a top row and join all cells.
   E. Change the bottom line of the new top row to a thick line.
   F. Center the heading All-Sports Shoe Company, Inc.
   G. Add a bottom row.
   H. Remove the column lines in the last row.
   I. In the last row, type "Total Inventory" at the left edge and at the right edge add the sum of the Total column.
   J. Print the document.
2. Exit WordPerfect.

12

Equations

The objectives of this lesson are to

- Form an equation
- Use the equation menu
- Use the equation option menu
- Form and insert special characters and symbols
- Position the equation within the graphics box
- Position the graphics box between the left and right margins

Writing Equations

If you need to include equations when you write reports, magazine or journal articles, and other related documents, WordPerfect's Equation feature can be extremely useful. The Equation feature allows you to insert a picture of a mathematical model as a graphic. Note that this equation is merely a picture of an equation and does not actually perform any mathematical computations.

To create an equation in graphics format, you would position the cursor at the point in the document where you intend to insert the equation and

1. . . . . Press **[Alt]+[F9]** to use the Graphics command.
2. . . . . Press **6** to select Equation.
3. . . . . Press **1** to select Create.
4. . . . . Press **9** to select Edit.
5. . . . . Write your equation.
   Use the Guidelines for Equation Writing given in the section below.

You can view the results of your typed commands in the top window of the Equation Editor by pressing **[Ctrl]+[F3]** at any point in the process. Press **[Ctrl]+[F3]** a second time to return to the lower window where you are typing the equation.

6. . . . .Press **[F7] [F7]** to exit the Equation Editor feature and return to the document.

Following Guidelines for Writing Equations

When you write equations, you must follow certain guidelines to ensure that your equations adhere to the proper format. Remember that

1. The equation will be centered on its own line within the page of text unless you specify another alignment.
2. The WordPerfect Equation Editor closely follows the specific verbalized language for describing a mathematical equation. If you were to describe the following equation to someone,

$$y = \frac{1}{\sqrt{x}}$$

   "y equals one over the square root of x."
   To describe to the WordPerfect Equation Editor what you want written, you would type,

   y = 1 over sqrt x

3. The letters in the equation are lowercase, and each command is one space apart. The space can be an actual space or a "phantom" space (see the next guideline).
4. You can create a phantom space by placing the tilde (~) between the commands. This use of the tilde in the command results in a space in the printed equation. For example, the command

   y~=~1 over sqrt x; **or** y~=~1 OVER SQRT x

   will create the equation

$$y = \frac{1}{\sqrt{x}}$$

   Note that the word commands are **not** case sensitive **unless** the command is written to represent an upper or lowercase **Greek** letter.
   You can insert a thin space by using the backward accent (‘). A thin space is one-fourth of the normal space width. Two backward accents would result in a half-space.
5. You can either type the commands, symbols, numbers, and variables required to write a mathematical equation, as in the above equation, or you can select them from the Equation Palette. Once you are familiar with the language of the Equation Editor, you will probably find it much easier and faster to type the characters than to select them from the palette. You will find some characters only on the keyboard. However, if you cannot remember the exact word or phrase to type, you may find the menus helpful.
   The procedure for using the Equation Palette is given below.

To use the Equation Palette, you would first follow the instructions for writing equations given at the beginning of this chapter, and then

1.....Press **[F5]** to switch to Palette.
2.....Press **[PgUp]** or **[PgDn]** to locate the desired page (menu) in the Palette.
After moving the cursor to the desired command or symbol, you would
3.....Press **[Enter]** to insert the command or symbol into the equation.
Pressing **[Enter]** automatically inserts a space at the end of the command or symbol, and returns control to the keyboard for typed entries.
If you wanted to continue using the palette, you would
4.....Repeat steps 2 and 3 as many times as necessary to form the complete equation.
5.....Press **[F7]** twice to return to the document.
The Equation Palette does not contain the alphabetic characters (A-Z), the digits (0-9), or an equal sign (=). However, you can type these symbols from the keyboard. The advantage of the Equation Palette is that it allows you to select symbols that you cannot easily form using the normal keyboard.
To expedite equation writing use Table 12-1, which lists the keywords needed to translate the most frequently used equation characters.
In the following exercise, you will use the Equation Palette to write the equation

$$y=\frac{1}{\sqrt{x}}$$

1.....Press **[Alt]+[F9], 6, 1, 9** to begin the equation-writing process.
2.....Type **y = 1** (making sure to leave a space after the 1).
3.....Press **[F5]** to switch to the palette on the right side of the screen.
Position the highlighted cursor over the command OVER and
4.....Press **[Enter]** to add the OVER command to the equation.
The program automatically adds a space to the end of the command and switches you back to normal keyboard entry.
5.....Press **[F5]** to switch back to the Palette option.
Position the highlighted cursor over the SQRT command and
6.....Press **[Enter]** to add the SQRT command to the equation.
7.....Type **x** to finish the equation.
8.....Press **[F7]** twice to leave the equation-writing process.

6. Some commands not given in Table 12-1 require a more detailed explanation. For example, you can see the importance of using braces {} in the following two equations:
If you type x + 1 over x - 2, the result is

$$\mathrm{x}+\frac{1}{x}-2$$

Mathematic Equation Writing Reference Chart

Symbol	Keyword	Description
$\sum$	SUM	Summation
∑	SMALLSUM	Small summation
(	(	Left parenthesis
)	)	Right parenthesis
[	[	Left bracket
]	]	Right bracket
$\vert$	LINE	Vertical line
→	VEC	Vector above: x VEC = x
‾	BAR	Overline: x BAR = $\bar{x}$
^	HAT	Hat above: x HAT = $\hat{x}$
~	TILDE	Tilde above: x TILDE = $\tilde{x}$
′	'	Prime
″	"	Double prime
∞	INF	Infinity
·	CDOT	Single, centered dot
⋯	DOTSAXIS	Ellipsis (centered)
…	DOTSLOW	Ellipsis (on baseline)
∂	PARTIAL	Partial derivative
x	TIMES	Multiplication sign
÷	DIV	Division sign
±	PLUSMINUS	Plus or minus
±	+-	Plus or minus
≤	<=	Less than or equal to
≥	>=	Greater than or equal to
≠	!=	Not equal
≈	APPROX	Approximately equal to
°	DEG	Degree

Symbol	Greek Letter Keyword (case specific)
α	alpha
β	beta
ε	varepsilon
Δ	DELTA
λ	lambda
μ	mu
π	pi
σ	sigma
Σ	SIGMA

Words which retain the case in which they are entered		
	Keyword	**Description**
	ln	Natural logarithm
	lim	Limit
	min	Minimum
	MIN	Minimum
	max	Maximum
	MAX	Maximum

Table 12-1: *Mathematic Equation Reference Chart*

Braces will change the form of the equation. If you now write { x + 1 } over { x - 2 }, the resulting equation is

$$\frac{x+1}{x-2}$$

7. You can use the command OVERSM in the equation x+ ½ – 2 to change the dimensions of the number "1 OVER x." The keystrokes remain the same, but the command (OVER) is changed to OVERSM. Changing the command produces a reduced ½:

$$x + {\scriptstyle \frac{1}{2}} - 2$$

8. You can write subscripts and superscripts either as SUB or SUP before the number; or you can identify them by using the underscore character (_) for the subscript and the hat character (^) for the superscript. If you require both a subscript and a superscript, the hierarchy for using subscripts and superscripts is subscript to superscript: SUB then SUP, or _ then ^. You can write equations that contain only subscripts, or only superscripts, or that contain both.

   You can write the equation x_1^2 as

   x SUB 1 SUP 2; or as x _ 1 ^ 2

   Note that the subscript **must** come before the superscript.

9. FROM and TO are commands that provide beginning and ending symbol limits. If you require both beginning and ending symbol limits the hierarchy to follow is bottom to top, FROM then TO. You can write an equation using only a beginning symbol limit or only an ending symbol limit.

   You would use the following keystrokes to set beginning and ending symbol limits. Note that the FROM **must** come before the TO.

   SUM FROM { k = 0 } TO INF

$$\sum_{k=0}^{\infty}$$

Quick Reference Guide for Commands

Command	Example	Description
# (pound sign)	a # b	Used to separate rows; similar to the Enter key.
& (ampersand)	r & s	Used to align rows of equations vertically by (1) column in MATRIX and MATFORM or by (2) character.
. (period)	RIGHT .	Used with dynamic operators to indicate either a no opening or a no closing delimiter.
\ (backslash)	\‘	Treat the following command as a literal.
‘ (backward accent)	A‘‘B	Creates a thin space. Can use in series to create several thin spaces. Thin space is 25 percent of normal.
{ (left brace)	OVER {	Indicates the beginning of a group.
} (right brace)	} RIGHT	Indicates the end of a group.
~ (tilde)	~=~	Creates a space.
ALIGNC	ALIGNC a	A default command centering a group.
ALIGNL	ALIGNL a	Aligns argument at left margin of group or subgroup.
ALIGNR	ALIGNR a	Aligns argument at right margin of group or subgroup.
BINOM	BINOM a b	Creates a binomial construction.
BINOMSM	BINOMSM a b	Similar to BINOM except printed in smaller font.
BOLD	BOLD a	Causes the argument to be bolded.
FROM	FROM 1 TO j	Used to identify a beginning limit for SUM or INT.
FUNC	FUNC name	Causes any variable to be treated as a function name. Variable will be printed in base font.
HORZ	HORZ x	Manual adjusting of horizontal spacing. Increments of .012 inches.
ITAL	ITAL P	Italicizes the argument.
LEFT	LEFT DLINE	Indicates a dynamic delimiter followed by one of the following delimiters: (/ [DLINE LANGLE LBRACE LCEIL LFLOOR LINE. A RIGHT command must always be used with a LEFT command.
MATFORM	MATFORM { ALIGNx & ALIGNx & ··· & ALIGNx }	Used to indicate alignment in a MATRIX command.
MATRIX	MATRIX { a & b # m & n }	Creates a matrix of the equation statement.

NROOT	NROOT n a	Creates an nth root graphic.
OVER	a OVER b	Used to create fractions.
OVERLINE	OVERLINE a	Creates a bar over the top of the argument.
OVERSM	a OVERSM b	Same as OVER but printed in smaller font.
PHANTOM	PHANTOM a	Used to align similar characters over one another in multiple line graphics.
RIGHT	RIGHT DLINE	Must be used with LEFT command and its similar delimiter of :) /] DLINE RANGLE RBRACE RCEIL RFLOOR LINE.
SQRT	SQRT a	Creates a square root graphic sign.
STACK	STACK { a # b }	Aligns sets of groups or subgroups over each other.
STACKALIGN	STACKALIGN { a & b # r & s }	Similar to STACK except an arbitrary symbol is used for alignment.
SUB or _	a SUB b	Used to create a subscript b of a.
SUP or ^	r SUB s	Used to create a superscript s of r.
TO	FROM i TO j	Used to establish the upper limit for SUM or INT.
UNDERLINE	UNDERLINE a	Used to underscore an argument.
VERT	VERT a	Similar to HORZ. Used for vertical alignment.

Table 12-2: *Quick Reference Guide for Commands*

10. If you find the dimension of the SUM or SIGMA too large for your equation, you can reduce the size simply by using the command SMALLSUM instead of SUM. Using the above example, the command

    SMALLSUM FROM { k = 0 } TO INF

    produces the equation

$$\sum_{k=0}^{\infty}$$

11. When you want to find the root of an equation other than the square root, you can specify the command NROOT. The NROOT command also follows a hierarchy: you must execute it from left to right. The command NROOT must first be followed by the number representing the nth root, and then the variable.

    To represent the following equation:

$$x=\sqrt[3]{-\frac{27}{8}}$$

    You would write the following command:

    x = NROOT 3 { - { 27 OVER 8 } }

If you desired spacing around the equal sign, you would insert the phantom space (~):

x~=~NROOT 3 { - { 27 OVER 8 } }

to obtain the result:

$$x = \sqrt[3]{-\frac{27}{8}}$$

Inserting Common Operators and Symbols

The palette does not include a number of common arithmetic operators. You will find it easier and faster to use the keyboard to insert these common arithmetic operators and symbols than to access the palette tables. The omitted operators and symbols are

+ - * / = < > ! ? . | @ " , :

Using Dynamic Delimiters

Six delimiters automatically change in size to fit the equation. These delimiters can change in length or height or both. The six are OVER, SQRT, NROOT, LEFT (parenthesis or bracket), RIGHT (parenthesis or bracket), and BINOM.

The OVER delimiter operates as the line separating the numerator and the denominator in an equation. In the following equation:

$$\frac{12 \cdot 11 \cdot 10 \cdot 9!}{9!} = 1320$$

the typed equation is as follows:

{ 1 2~cdot~1 1~cdot~1 0~cdot~9 ! } over { 9 ! }~=~1 3 2 0

The SQRT delimiter represents the square root sign. The NROOT appears to be similar but has a specific stated root value. Using the following two equations as examples:

$$\sqrt{\frac{2}{x}} \text{ and } \sqrt[rt]{\frac{2}{x}}$$

the two typed equations are as follows:

SQRT { 2 over x } and

NROOT { r t } { 2 over x }

The LEFT and RIGHT delimiters are similar to the left and right parentheses. However, the LEFT and RIGHT delimiters can increase in height while the parentheses cannot. The appropriate symbol (parenthesis or square bracket) must follow the LEFT and RIGHT delimiter. In the following equation:

$$\left[\frac{(\frac{\rho}{\lambda})^s}{(\frac{\mu}{\lambda})} \right]$$

the typed equation is as follows:

[LEFT [{ LEFT ({ ital rho over lambda } RIGHT) sup s over { LEFT ({ mu over lambda } RIGHT) } RIGHT]

The BINOM delimiter creates the following graphic from the command of BINOM x y.

$$\binom{x}{y}$$

Forming Special Characters

Some of the characters that you may wish to insert into an equation may not be found on the keyboard or in the equation tables. WordPerfect has many sets of characters and symbols that you can access for insertion into a document. These sets include Box Drawing (Character Set 3), Typographic Symbols (Character Set 4), Iconic Symbols (Character Set 5), Hebrew (Character Set 9), Cyrillic (Character Set 10), or Hiragana and Katakana (Character Set 11).

You can use the Compose command **[Ctrl] + [V]** to form and insert these distinct characters and symbols into a document. By using the Equation feature, you can also place these same characters and symbols into a graphics box.

To form the following equation without a file in current memory:

$$F_X(b) = P\{X(\omega) \le b\}$$

1.....Press **[Ctrl]+[V]** to access the Compose feature.
2.....Press **5,21 [Enter]** to select character number 21, the right-pointing hand, from Character Set 5. (Because this is a graphic, a gray box may appear instead of right-pointing hand.)

Save the file on the student data disk as A:TESTNO_1.

You are now ready to create an equation where the right-pointing hand is a part of the graphics.

1.....Press **[Alt]+[F9], 6, 1, 1** to select the file into which you will type this equation graphic.
2.....Press **[F5]**
Select TESTNO_1 from the list on the student data disk or type **A:TESTNO_1 [Enter]** to retrieve the file from the student data disk.
3.....Press **9** to select the Edit option.
4.....Move the cursor to the right of the symbol and type the equation as shown on the previous page.
5.....Press **[Enter]** twice to return to the document.

Justifying Equations

The placement of equations in a document is important. You can generally achieve satisfactory placement of the equation by using one of two methods for justifying them. Depending on the circumstances, you may find that one method is easier than the other. You can justify the equation within the graphics box, or you can justify the graphics box itself. In both instances, justification can be left, right, or centered.

Justifying the equation within the box is probably the easiest method when you want flush right, flush left, or centered justification. You can easily accomplish this justification by creating a graphics box using the commands **[Alt]+[F9], 6, 1**. This method creates a default box width extending from the left margin to the right margin, and automatically scales the box height to fit the equation.

Within this default box, you can justify the equation to the left, the right, or center it by changing the initial settings through the Setup command. You can change the internal justification of the equation when you create the equation or when you edit the equation.

The easiest way to left-justify the equation within the default box is to go to the Equation Editor. Use the Setup option from the following lower menu:

Screen Redisplay; **List** Commands; **Switch** Window; **Setup** Options

1.....Press **[Shift]+[F1]** to select the Setup Option.
From the Equation options,
2.....Press **3** to select Horizontal Alignment.
From the new menu

Horizontal Alignment: 1 Left; **2 C**enter; **3 R**ight: 0

3.....Press **1** to select Left justification.
4.....Press **[Enter]** to return to the Equation Editor.

The equation that you created or edited after executing the above steps would be left-justified within the default box until you change the horizontal settings. You can horizontally realign the contents of any previously created equation box by changing the settings using the procedure outlined above.

You can change the internal horizontal alignment to a desired justification for all subsequent boxes by going to the Initial Settings option. In the following exercise you will select left justification.

Clear the screen.

1.....Press **[Shift]+[F1]** to select the Setup Menu.
2.....Press **4** to select Initial Settings.
3.....Press **3** to select Equations.
4.....Press **3** to select Horizontal Alignment.
From the menu

Horizontal Alignment: 1 Left; **2 C**enter; **3 R**ight: 0

5.....Press **1** to select Left justification.
6.....Press **[Enter]** three times to return to the document.

Any equations that you create now will be left-justified within the default box until you change the initial settings.

The following equation shows the results of using the left justification option:

$$\sum_i x_{ik} - \sum_j x_{kj} = 0, \quad \text{for } k = 2, 3, \cdots, N-1$$

If you use center justification (option 2), the equation will be placed as follows:

$$\sum_i x_{ik} - \sum_j x_{kj} = 0, \quad \text{for } k = 2, 3, \cdots, N-1$$

If you use right justification (option 3), the equation will now be positioned:

$$\sum_i x_{ik} - \sum_j x_{kj} = 0, \quad \text{for } k = 2, 3, \cdots, N-1$$

General Exercises

1. Center the equations under the following excerpts:
   A. The maximal flow problem can be formulated as a Linear Programming problem where the conservation of flow constraint is

$$\sum_i x_{ik} - \sum_j x_{kj} = 0, \quad \text{for } k = 2, 3, \cdots, N-1$$

   B. If the other assumptions of the model are retained, it has been found that, when s = 1,

$$W_k = \frac{1/\mu}{B_{k-1} \cdot B_k}, \quad \text{for } k = 1, 2, \cdots, N,$$

   which is the solution for the preemptive service case.

   C. Additionally, it has been determined that if Xj, the steady state expected waiting time for an associate of priority class j, is:

$$X_j = 1 - \frac{\sum_{i=1}^{j} \lambda_i}{s\mu}, \quad \text{for } k = 1, 2, \cdots, N,$$

   the results will be the same. The recursive relationships involve probabilities.

   D. The recursive relationships which these probabilities satisfy are shown in the following model:

$$f_{ij}^{(n)} = p_{ij}^{(n)} - f_{ij}^{(1)} p_{jj}^{(n-1)} - \cdots - f_{ij}^{(n-1)} p_{jj}$$

E. Using these probabilities, the revised simplex method can be used to compute x_{ij}, where the results for all cases will be determined as:

$$\begin{bmatrix} x'_{1j} \\ x'_{2j} \\ \cdot \\ \cdot \\ x'_{mj} \end{bmatrix} = \mathbf{A}^{-1} B_j$$

2. Left-justify the equations in problems 1a-1e.
3. Create as one document problems 1a-1e. Center the equations.
4. If you intend to go on to another set of exercises, clear the screen. If not, exit WordPerfect.

Course-Specific Exercises

Group A Accounting

1. Load WordPerfect if necessary. Construct and center the following equations:

   A. $\frac{12!}{9!} = \frac{12 \cdot 11 \cdot 10 \cdot 9!}{9!} = 1320$

   B. $p = a'/b' - (1/b')Q_d$

   C. $p(\mu - 2\sigma \leq y \leq \mu + 2\sigma)$

   D. $d = \frac{1}{d'} = \frac{\Delta P}{\Delta Q_s}$

   E. $f(x) = a_0 + a_1 x + a_2 x^2 + a_3 x^3 + \cdots + a_n x^n$

   Save the equations as ACTG_EQU.
2. Left-justify the equations in the ACTG_EQU file and print the new file.
3. Center the above equations and place the following boxes around each:

Equation	**Type of box**
A.	Single line
B.	Double line
C.	A thick bottom line only, margin to margin
D.	Dashed lines, top and bottom only
E.	Extra-thick on ends only

   Print the equations with the specified boxes.
4. If you intend to go on to another set of exercises, clear the screen. If not, exit WordPerfect.

Group B Marketing

1. Load WordPerfect if necessary. Construct and center the following equations:

A. $S_\infty = \frac{a_1}{1-r}, \; |r|<1$

B. $S_t = \alpha D_t + (1-\alpha)S_{t-1}$

C. $SD = \sqrt{\frac{\sum_{t=1}^{n} (E_t^2)}{n-1}}$

D. $MAPE = \frac{\sum_{t=1}^{n} \left(\frac{|E_t|}{D_t}\right) \times 100\%}{n}$

E. $MSE = \frac{\sum_{t=1}^{n} (E_t)^2}{n}$

Save the equations as MKTG_EQU.

2. Left-justify the equations in the MKTG_EQU file and print the new file.
3. Center the above equations and place the following boxes around each:

Equation	Type of box
A.	Dotted line
B.	Double line top and bottom only, margin to margin
C.	A thick top line only, margin to margin
D.	Single lines, top and bottom only
E.	Extra-thick on ends only

Print the equations with the specified boxes.

4. If you intend to go on to another set of exercises, clear the screen. If not, exit WordPerfect.

Group C Finance

1. Load WordPerfect if necessary. Construct and center the following equations:

A. $Q_d = a' - b'p$

B. $\frac{\partial L}{\partial x_2} = \frac{\partial y}{\partial x_2} - \lambda g \frac{\partial g}{\partial x_2} - \lambda h \frac{\partial h}{\partial x_2} = 0$

C. $\bar{y} \pm t_{.025} \left(\frac{S}{\sqrt{n}}\right)$

D. $\left(\frac{a}{b}\right)^m = \frac{a^m}{b^m}, \; b \neq 0$

E. $$\text{MAD} = \frac{\sum_{t=1}^{n} (E_t^2)}{n}$$

Save the equations as FIN_EQU.

2. Left-justify the equations in the FIN_EQU file and print the new file.
3. Center the above equations and place the following boxes around each:

Equation	**Type of box**
A.	Thick line
B.	Dashed line
C.	A thick bottom line only, margin to margin
D.	Single line, top and bottom only, margin to margin
E.	Extra-thick on ends only

Print the equations with the specified boxes.

4. If you intend to go on to another set of exercises, clear the screen. If not, exit WordPerfect.

Group D Production

1. Load WordPerfect if necessary. Construct and center the following equations:

A. $$d' = \frac{\Delta Q_S}{\Delta P}$$

B. $$\sigma_{CF} = \sqrt{\sum_{i=1}^{n} P_i[CF_i - E(CF_i)]^2}$$

C. $$\text{EOQ} = \sqrt{\frac{2 \text{ x YD x } O_C}{\text{UP x IF}}}$$

D. $$\frac{1}{T_{TOTAL}} = \frac{1}{T_{RM}} + \frac{1}{T_{WIP}} + \frac{1}{T_{FGI}}$$

E. $$\sigma_{CP} = \sqrt{(\sigma_{act}) + (\sigma_{act}) + \cdots + (\sigma_{act})}$$

Save the equations as PROD_EQU.

2. Left-justify the equations in the PROD_EQU file and print the new file.
3. Center the above equations and place the following boxes around each:

Equation	**Type of box**
A.	Dotted line
B.	Double line
C.	Extra-thick bottom line only, margin to margin
D.	Dashed lines, top and bottom only
E.	Extra-thick on ends only

Print the equations with the specified boxes.

4. Exit WordPerfect.

APPENDIX

The appendix includes copies of three sample letters that are used in the exercises in this book.

Sample Letter A

September 16, 1990

Ms. Alice Heldt
100 Battalion Blvd.
Newburgh, NY 10996-1797

Dear Ms. Heldt:

Our records show your phone number to be 345-5432. If this has changed, please inform us immediately by calling this toll-free number: 1-(800) 897-3777.

Congratulations! You are a winner in the Lott-a-America Sweepstakes and are soon to be the recipient of a check for $5,000,000.00 and an additional bonus of a Lamborghini Countach.

The deadline for claiming your prizes is one year from the date of this letter. An Internal Revenue Agent will have to be present when you claim your prizes.

As the winner of the Lott-a-America Sweepstakes, your name is public information and cannot be withheld from the press. If you wish, you can have an attorney claim the prizes in your behalf to avoid the Television and Press.

Please keep this form for your records.

Yours truly,

Megan Maura
Sweepstakes Director

Sample Letter B

Aromax Corporation
1721 North Pierce Street
Grand Junction, Colorado 81501

Dear Aromax Employees:

Your current Employee Health Care Card will expire on December 31, 1990. With the enclosed card, we are extending your current Employee Health Care Card through June 30, 1991.

Due to our upcoming move to Colorado Springs early next year, we will not be issuing new Employee Health Care cards at this time. The new cards will be issued prior to June 30, 1991.

Should you have any questions regarding the Health Care Cards or your extension, please call (303) 248-6171 between 8:00 a.m. and 5:30 p.m.

Thank you for your cooperation.

Sincerely,

Health Care Claims
Administration

Sample Letter C

Aromax Corporation
1721 North Pierce Street
Grand Junction, Colorado 81501

Dear Aromax Employees:

Effective January 1, 1991 in accordance with the Consolidated Omnibus Budget Reconciliation Act of 1985 the company will offer new extended coverage for the:

1) Employee Health Care Plan for all exempt and non-exempt employees at Aromax.
2) Dependent Health Care Plan for all married couples employed by Aromax.
3) Vision Care Plan for employees and dependents.

How Extended Coverage Works

You and your dependents may have coverage expanded from 18 months if any of the following "qualifying events" occur:

Your employment with Aromax is terminated for any reason other than gross misconduct, or you are laid off;

Your employment classification changes from **New Normal** or **Regular**, to **Part Time**, **Intermittent**, or **Temporary**; or

You retire with less than 10 years of service with the Company (If you were hired on or after August 1, 1989).

Should you have any questions regarding your extension, please call (303) 248-6171 between 8:00 a.m. and 5:30 p.m.

Sincerely,

Health Care Claims
Administration

INDEX

References to figures are printed in boldface type. References to tables are in italics.

NOTES

NOTES

NOTES

NOTES

NOTES

NOTES

NOTES

NOTES

NOTES

NOTES

NOTES